Into the Future:
The Foundation of Library and Information
Services in the Post-Industrial Era,
Second Edition

Contemporary Studies in Information Management, Policy, and Services
(formerly Information Management, Policy, and Services series)

Peter Hernon, series editor

Technology and Library Information Services
  Carol Anderson and Robert Hauptman, 1993
Information Policies
  Robert H. Burger, 1993
Organizational Decision Making and Information Use
  Mairéad Browne, 1993
Seeking Meaning: A Process Approach to Library and Information Services
  Carol Collier Kuhlthau, 1993
Meaning and Method in Information Studies
  Ian Cornelius, 1996
Library Performance Accountability and Responsiveness Essays in Honor of Ernest R. DeProspo
  Charles C. Curran and F. William Summers, 1990
Curriculum Initiative: An Agenda and Strategy for Library Media Programs
  Michael B. Eisenberg and Robert E. Berkowitz, 1988
Resource Companion to Curriculum Initiative: An Agenda and Strategy for Library Media Programs
  Michael B. Eisenberg and Robert E. Berkowitz, 1988
Information Problem-Solving: The Big Six Skills Approach to Library & Information Skills Instruction
  Michael B. Eisenberg and Robert E. Berkowitz, 1990
Deep Information: The Role of Information Policy in Environmental Sustainability
  John Felleman, 1977
Database Ownership and Copyright Issues Among Automated Library Networks: An Analysis and Case Study
  Janice R. Franklin, 1993
Research for School Library Media Specialists
  Kent R. Gustafson and Jane Bandy Smith, 1994
The Role and Importance of Managing Information for Competitive Positions in Economic Development
  Keith Harman, 1989

A Practical Guide to Managing Information for Competitive Positioning to Economic Development
    Keith Harman, 1990
Into the Future: The Foundations of Library and Information Services in the Post-Industrial Era
    Michael H. Harris and Stan A. Hannah, 1993
Into the Future: The Foundations of Library and Information Services in the Post-Industrial Era, Second Edition
    Michael H. Harris, Stan A. Hannah, and Pamela C. Harris, 1998
Librarianship: The Erosion of a Woman's Profession
    Roma Harris, 1992
Statistics: A Component of the Research Process, Second Edition
    Peter Hernon, 1994
Research Misconduct: Issues, Implications and Strategies
    Ellen Altman and Peter Hernon, 1997
Service Quality in Academic Libraries
    Peter Hernon and Ellen Altman, 1996
Microcomputer Software and Performing Statistical Analysis: A Handbook for Supporting Library Decision Making
    Peter Hernon and john V. Richardson (Editors), 1988
Evaluation and Library Decision Making
    Peter Hernon and Charles R. McClure, 1990
Public Access to Government Information, Second Edition
    Peter Hernon and Charles R. McClure, 1988
Federal Information Policies in the 1990s: Views and Perspectives
    Peter Hernon and Charles R. McClure, 1988
Statistics for Library Decision Making: A Handbook
    Peter Hernon, et al., 1989
Understanding Information Retrieval Interactions: Theoretical and Practical Implications
    Carol A. Hert, 1997
Reclaiming the American Library Past: Writing the Women In
    Suzanne Hildenbrand (Editor), 1996
Libraries: Partners in Adult Literacy
    Deborah Johnson, Jane Robbins, and Douglas L. Zweizig, 1991
The National Research and Education Network 9NREN): Research and Policy Perspectives
    Charles R. McClure, Ann P. Bishop, Philip Doty and Howard Rosenbaum (editors), 1991
Library and Information Science Research: Perspective and Strategies for Improvement
    Charles R. McClure and Peter Hernon (editors), 1991

U.S. Government Information Policies: Views and Perspectives
  Charles R. McClure, Peter Hernon, and Harold C. Relyea, 1989
U.S. Scientific and Technical Information Policies: Views and Perspectives
  Charles R. McClure and Peter Hernon, 1989
Gatekeepers in Ethnolinguistic Communities
  Cheryl Metoyer-Duran, 1993
Knowledge Diffusion in the U.S. Aerospace Industry: Managing Knowledge for Competitive Advantage
  Thomas E. Pinelli, et al., 1997
Basic Research Methods for Librarians, Third Edition
  Ronald R. Powell, 1997
Information of the Image, Second Edition
  Allan Pratt, 1997
Silencing Science: National Security Controls and Scientific Communication
  Harold C. Relyea, 1994
Records Management and the Library: Issues and Practices
  Candy Schwartz and Peter Hernon, 1993
Assessing the Public Library Planning Process
  Annabel K. Stephens, 1996
Depository Library Use of Technology: A Practitioner's Perspective
  Jan Swanbeck and Peter Hernon, 1993
For Information Specialists
  Howard White, Marcia Bates, and Patrick Wilson, 1992
Public Library Youth Services: A Public Policy Approach
  Holly G. Willett, 1995

In Preparation:

The Dissemination of Spatial Data: A North American-European Comparative Study on the Impact of Government Information Policy
  Xavier Lopez
Silencing Scientists and Scholars in Other Fields: Power Paradigm Controls, Peer Review, and Scholarly Communication
  Gordon Moran
Computer-Supported Decision Making: Meeting the Decision Demands of Modern Organizations
  Charles L. Smith, Sr.
The Information Systems of International Inter-Governmental Organizations: A Reference Guide
  Robert Williams

Into the Future:
The Foundation of Library and Information Services in the Post-Industrial Era,
Second Edition

by
Michael H. Harris,
Stan A. Hannah,
and Pamela C. Harris

Ablex Publishing Corporation
Greenwich, Connecticut
London, England

Second Printing 1998

Printed in the United States of America

Library of Congress Cataloging-in-Publication Data

Harris, Michael H.
     Into the future : the foundations of library and information
services in the post-industrial era / by Michael H. Harris, Stan A.
Hannah, and Pamela C. Harris.—2nd ed.
        p.   cm.—(Contemporary studies in information management,
policy, and services)
    Includes bibliographical references (p.   ) index.
    ISBN 1-56750-354-3 (cloth).—ISBN 1-56750-355-1 (paper)
    1. Library science. 2. Information science. 3. Information
society. 4. Library science—United States. 5. Information
science—United States. 6. Information society—United States.
I. Hannah, Stan A. II. Harris, Pamela C. III. Title. IV. Series.

    020'.973—dc21   97-32488
                                                            CIP

Ablex Publishing Corporation
55 Old Post Road #2
P.O. Box 5297
Greenwich, CT 06830

Published in the U.K. and Europe by:.
JAI Press Ltd.
38 Tavistock Street
Covent Garden
London WC2E 7PB
England

Contents

Preface

Everthing should be made as simple as possible, but not simpler.

Albert Einstein

In 1962, Daniel Bell, the prominent Harvard sociologist, began to distribute and discuss a draft paper in which he outlined what was to become arguably the dominant metaphor of our age. By the time his famous book, *The Coming of Post-Industrial Society,* was published in 1973, Bell's original paper had already earned the title of the "most cited (and pirated) paper in sociology" and Bell (in 1970) had earned a place at the top of a list of America's 10 "most influential intellectuals" (Steinfels, 1979, chapter 7). At the same time the significant early warning of Bell's "second coming" was so extensive that his numerous critics were ready and waiting for the publication of his book-length explication of his famous construct. Since the original paper's appearance in 1962 to the present, the idea of a "post-industrial" or "information" society has been the subject of intense and often extremely insightful analysis by friend and foe alike from a wide range of disciplines.

Unfortunately, however, the library profession, which was to be infected by its own peculiarly virulent form of the post-industrial society metaphor in the form of F. W. Lancaster's "paperless society," was apparently proceeding in its own discussions of the implications of Bell's powerful metaphor without benefit of knowledge or understanding of the critical debate in the broader context. This lack of attention to the wide-ranging interdisciplinary literature on the subject of the post-industrial society and its implications for library and information services is clearly apparent in the impoverished and incestuous nature of the literature of library and information science dealing with the future of library and information service in these changing times.

The book before you undertakes the not immodest task of remedying this "blindspot" in the way in which librarians and information scientists think about the future of library and information service in the United States. Our purpose is to survey and assess critically the massive interdisciplinary literature on the "information society" and its implications for library and information service. It is our belief that Bell's vision has taken on some of the characteristics of a "self-fulfilling prophecy" in both the society at large and in our small corner of the information industry in America. If library and information scientists are to make critical progress in their attempts to understand the present and plan for the future, they must come to grips with the significant body of literature dealing with the issue, especially that second generation of scholarship that has appeared over the past decade.

Throughout we attempt to deal fairly, but critically, with the various viewpoints and ideological positions reflected in the post-industrial society literature. Wherever possible we have attempted to let the principals in the debate speak for themselves, and we have quoted extensively from the most representative work. Since one of our principle objectives is to present librarians with a broader and more informed foundation from which to consider their own future in the post-industrial society, we deploy a wide range of literature in the text, and in the bibliography.

Finally, unlike some of the early prophets of the post-industrial society, and yes, even our own paperless library cheerleaders, we do not consider this work to be the last word on the subject. How could it be, when the debate is still so intensely pursued, and the outcome so fiercely contested? But we feel that it is clearly time for library and information professionals to pause and take stock, and this work should be viewed as one collaborative attempt to contribute constructively to this collective stock-taking, as librarians and information professionals attempt to write their own job descriptions in the information age.

This is a genuinely collaborative work. First, it will be apparent to readers of this book that we have relied heavily on an extensive body of published literature. This deliberate attempt to confront the interdisciplinary literature on the post-industrial era and its implications for library and information services in America was greatly aided by the sophistication and comprehensiveness of the published literature. Second, we would like to thank the hundreds of students who have listened to parts, and finally all, of this book in the form of lectures in two courses taught by the authors. Finally, we owe a considerable debt to our editor, Peter Hernon. He both encouraged us to pursue our desire to try and understand the role of library and information services in the post-industrial era, and provided us with very useful guidance in every step of the process.

For the second edition of *Into the Future* we have revised a considerable amount of the book, and have actually shortened it by nearly 20 pages. The long, detailed endnotes and redundant passages have been deleted, and a significant number of now dated references have been dropped from the bibliography. At the same time, a considerable amount of new material has been added as we attempted to deal carefully with important subjects such as national communication policy under the Clinton administration in chapter 3, or women in librarianship in chapter 5. Many of these changes were made in the light of constructive criticism made by the librarians who reviewed the book when it first appeared. And yet, while much has changed, much has also remained the same. And we are convinced that the issues raised in *Into the Future* remain vital to any enlightened discussion of the role of librarians and libraries in the 21st century.

Michael H. Harris
Stan A. Hannah
Pamela C. Harris
November 1997

1

The Information Age

Historians looking back on events from the perspective of many years often give names to eras that contemporaries living through those times never contemplated. . . . Today the case can be made that we do not have to wait for some future historian to name the age in which we are living: It is the information age. (p. xi)

Walter Wriston

THE FUTURISTS GLIMPSE THE NEW ERA

"Every historical period has its godword," notes Theodore Roszak (1986); "there was An Age of Faith, An Age of Reason, An Age of Discovery." Our age, Roszak points out, has "been nominated as the Age of Information" (p. 19; and see Lubar, 1993). And while Roszak is skeptical of the "loose and exuberant talk" that we encounter on all aspects of the information age, he readily admits that the idea has become the dominant metaphor of our era, "a unifying theme that holds so many powerful social forces together," and as such is worthy of our critical attention (p. x).

Shortly after World War II many influential social commentators began to sense a need for a new "godword" or metaphor to explain the dramatic changes sweeping across the social, political, and economic terrain of American society. As James Beniger (1986) graphically illustrates, literally dozens tried their hand at labeling the new age.

But certainly, no one has named our age with more force and influence than the Harvard sociologist Daniel Bell. It is to his "declaration" that we must turn if we are to make any progress in our attempt to understand the depth and extent of the idea of an information society as developed by a wide range of social thinkers, and if we are to confront this vision with a numerous and diverse group of critical interventions in the debate about the nature of the information society.

But how to begin? Perhaps we might start with the often repeated story of the undergraduate Daniel Bell being stopped in a hallway by one of his faculty mentors who firmly announced that it was time for the young Bell to choose his specialty, to which Bell promptly responded, "I specialize in generalizations" (Steinfels, 1979, p. 161). That bold commitment to the risky business of generalization and futurology, combined with an aggressive and uncommonly sharp intellect, served Daniel Bell very well indeed. By 1970, he had earned the distinction of being ranked as one of America's ten most influential intellectual leaders (Kadushin, 1974, p. 30). Much of that reknown was based on a project, first initiated in the early 1960s, which was designed to map what Bell speculated was a revolutionary break in the history of the West. This revolutionary change, explored from many angles, and with frequently contradictory results, bore spectacular fruit, in 1973, with the publication of his now famous work entitled *The Coming of Post-Industrial Society* (see also Bell, 1967a).

In that work, so much discussed and so often misread, Daniel Bell presented what one commentator has sharply defined as a "breathless" new totalizing vision of the future of American society wrapped in an "eye-opening" conceptual package (Fox, 1982, p. 69). Countless commentators have analyzed Bell's massive and abstruse book in an attempt to discover the explanation for its striking impact on elite public opinion, and ultimately its inordinate impact on public opinion and public policy. What all appear to agree on is the massive display of erudition pointing to "a comprehensive framework of viewing the movement of contemporary society, buttressed by a dense, almost overwhelming, display of facts and interpretation ranging from art to economy, from automation to education" (Steinfels, 1979, p. 164).

Yet another group of analysts points to the success with which Bell posits his vision as a massive break with the past, and in doing so points to a time when "everything is new, unprecedented . . . the study of the past thereby loses credibility" (Gillam, 1982, p. 78). The discursive effect of this, argues Mark Poster (1990, pp. 22-23), is "to deny the validity of positions rooted in the analysis of industrial society:"

> The theory of post-industrial society introduces a break in the strong sense, one that reduces to insignificance those social dimensions that precede the break. . . . The theorist of postindustrialism has thus redefined social reality, has reconstituted the field of analysis, making invalid areas of experience that are not characteristic of the new model.

In this way Bell was able to render his critics impotent, for every critique can be ruled irrelevant if it was couched in terms and interpretations typical of "industrial society." As Poster (1990, p. 25) notes, in this way Bell "is doing things to the reader" and "not merely transmitting knowledge." Bell (1989) himself confirmed this analysis when he insisted that "postindustrial society is not a projection or extrapolation of existing trends in Western society; it is a new principle of social-technical organization and ways of life" (p. 167).

All of these, and other, explanations for the remarkable success of Daniel Bell's work and the power of his metaphor of the post-industrial society, or as he variously called it the "information society," will be explored in detail later in this book. But at this point we must turn to a question that can no longer be left unanswered: What exactly was this new and controversial vision that has proven so influential (on post-industrialism generally see Kumar, 1995; Rose, 1991)?

THE COMING OF POST-INDUSTRIAL SOCIETY

All who have struggled with Bell's *The Coming of Post-Industrial Society* concur that it is extremely difficult to read, and this probably explains the extent to which it has been misread, and ultimately glossed. But, at the same time, a host of serious readers of that text acknowledge that what Daniel Bell proposes is a vision of a new age that constitutes a *total* break with the past. Of pivotal consequence in this new age is "a changeover from a goods-producing society to an information or knowledge society" (Bell, 1973a, p. 487). For Bell, "the post-industrial society is an information society, as industrial society is a goods-producing society" (p. 467). The big change, then, lies in the emergence of a dynamic new commodity—information.

Despite the size of *The Coming of Post-Industrial Society*, the detail provided was frequently overwhelmed by the frustrating complexity of the book. As a result we are, indeed, fortunate to have Bell's later, and more accessible, explications of his metaphor, and especially the often quoted and reprinted essay entitled "The Social Framework of the Information Society" (1980a). In that work he begins in a typically cautious fashion:

> In the coming century, the emergence of a new social framework of telecommunications may be decisive for the way in which economic and social exchanges are conducted, the way knowledge is created and retrieved, and the character of the occupations and work in which men engage. (p. 500)

Driven by computer technology, and embedded in the context of the post-industrial society, this new society will have three fundamental "dimensions":

- The change from a goods-producing to a service society;

- The centrality of the codification of theoretical knowledge; and
- The creation of a new "intellectual technology" as a key tool of systems analysis and decision theory. (p. 501)

Bell argues forcefully for the idea that in the post-industrial society information is "intellectual property" and a commodity that will be produced, bought, and sold on "markets" (p. 506). Contra Karl Marx, he then insists that in the post-industrial era, knowledge, not labor, is the source of value. "In that sense," Bell suggests, "just as capital and labour have been the central variables of industrial society, so information and knowledge are the crucial variables of postindustrial society" (p. 506).

Bell further suggests that the key to this emerging new era is the combination of telecommunications and computer technology, driven by a new "intellectual technology" which for him means something between artificial intelligence and expert systems. All of this taken together will allow the "management of organized complexity" which constitutes the fundamental need of modern society. "In that respect," Bell claims, "the computer is a tool for managing the mass society, since it is the mechanism that orders and processes the transactions whose huge number has been mounting almost exponentially because of the increase in social interactions" (p. 509). Ultimately Bell (1989) concludes that the new intellectual technology combined with computers represents "a set of changes that pervade all aspects of society and reorganize all older relationships" (p. 167). As Bell explained in the 1976 paperback edition of *The Coming of Post-Industrial Society*, "what a post-industrial transformation means is the enhancement of instrumental powers, powers over nature, and powers, even, over people" (p. xxi).

Clearly embedded in Bell's vision of the post-industrial society is a decidedly technocratic model of societal management. For an inevitable by-product of the rise of the post-industrial or information society will be the concomitant rise of a new class of information professionals dedicated to the impartial and rational management of society's problems. Implicit in this proposal is the assumption, long present in Bell's work (see Bell, 1960), that "the remaining social-political problems" have all become "technical questions for which technical solutions would be forthcoming" (Archer, 1990, p. 102).

Bell insisted that there was little to fear from the rise of this new class, and claimed that "the idea that the knowledge elite will become a new power elite seems to me to be exaggerated" (1980a, p. 542). He calmly notes that there is little evidence to suggest that "the knowledge elites will become a cohesive 'class'," for they are simply "too large and diffuse" (p. 543).

Also central to his vision (1989, p. 171) is the claim that we will witness the withering away of alienating industrial labor in the information society, and the rise of a healthier, more rewarding, and more productive style of work that will represent nearly utopian "games among persons":

If character is defined by work, then we shall see a society where 'nature' is largely excluded and 'things' are largely excluded within the experience of persons. If more and more individuals are in work situations that involve a 'game between persons', clearly more and more questions of equity and 'comparable worth' will arise. The nature of hierarchy in work may be increasingly questioned, and new modes of participation may be called for. All of these portend huge changes in the structures of organization from those we have seen in the older models.

And, finally, Bell (1980a) notes that the combination of the computer and telecommunications will strike hard at modes of communication characteristic of earlier eras. For it is apparent that we will witness the "reduction if not the elimination of paper in transactions and exchanges" and even, quite possibly, the elimination of the library as we have known it—it "may become a sad monument of the printed past" (pp. 533, 529).

Thus, we have come full circle, for now we see the vision more clearly: "The emergence of a new social framework" that will revolutionize the economy, the workplace, and even "social exchanges" among persons. Bell also leaves us with a threat and a promise. Given the inevitability of the emergence of post-industrial society we are presented with the threat: Ride the post-industrial wave or drown. For those luddites who still remain skeptical of his vision he pointedly responds: "Just ask the Japanese" (Bell, 1982, p. 86; see also Bowes, 1981; Ivy, 1988; Masuda, 1981). At the same time Bell (1980a, p. 545) leaves us with the promise of

alternative modes of achieving individuality and variety within a vastly increased output of goods. This is the promise—the fateful question is whether the promise will be realized.

ENTER THE CRITICS

Later in this chapter we discuss the spread and influence of the many permutations of the post-industrial society construct throughout every strata of American society. At this point it is necessary to examine the initial controversy and widespread debate that reverberated through intellectual circles as a result of the impact of Bell's brilliant theoretical intervention.

Given the extent and nature of the debate over the post-industrial society metaphor, one should not be surprised that many have undertaken the considerable task of classifying the responses to Bell's work. Those schemes designed to help us organize the imposing critical literature on the post-industrial metaphor vary considerably in their conclusions and organizing frameworks. For instance, Forester (1989a) suggests that it might be useful to organize the literature on the post-industrial society into two basic categories: Optimistic and pessimistic, or, as he puts it, "human choice" and "technological determinist" categories (p. 2). One model posed by Barry Jones points to two categories that reflect a different angle of vision. Jones (1982) sees the two groups as being those who view the post-industrial era as a fundamental break with the past—a "radical discontinuity," and those who insist that the post-industrial society is simply an instance in slow evolutionary change, and that what we are witnessing is nothing more than "traditional incrementalism."

Clearly, all of these schemes have value in helping us to organize the literature on the post-industrial society, and the readers of this book may find that their own understanding of the literature on libraries and information services in the information society corresponds nicely to one or more of the outlines presented above. However, since none of these schemes quite suits us, we offer our own categories in an attempt to organize the critical literature.

TECHNOLOGICAL DETERMINISM AND ITS CRITICS

"The supposed effects of the so-called 'information revolution'," notes Kees Brants (1989), "are, at least in part, an ideological construct in which different actors fulfill different roles in defining the reality of technological developments in such a way as to leave little room for deviating views" (p. 79). The tendency for visions of the information age to be stated in totalizing terms, in both their "promise and curse" models, is a central characteristic of the literature on the subject (Winston, 1986). Thus, one of the principal explanations for the extent and intensity of the debate on the information age must be located in the technological determinism so prevalent in the essential texts in the debate, what Langdon Winner (1986) refers to as recurrent themes of "technophilia" and "technophobia."

In a brilliant book on the subject of *Autonomous Technology* Winner (1977) notes that the idea that "technology is somehow out of control by human agency" has garnered a great deal of attention (p. 15). Winner points out that "technological determinism" is premised on two basic assumptions: "1) that the technical base of a society is the fundamental condition affecting all patterns of social existence and 2) that changes in technology are the single most important source of change in society" (p. 76). What Winner emphasizes, is that taken in this form, few theorists would take "unabashedly" deterministic positions. Yet, the evidence suggests that this has, indeed, been the case in much of the literature on the information society (Smith & Marx, 1994).

The idea that technology possesses uniquely redemptive powers has been the subject of intense scrutiny. In a book on "technological utopianism," Howard Segal (1985) documents the long history of the "belief in the inevitability of progress and in progress precisely as technological progress" (p. 1). He also argues for the view that such technological utopianism has great appeal for a society that is tempted to see "unprecedented technological progress as the panacea for unprecedented social problems" (pp. 7–8). We can now see that one of the most influential and controversial aspects of Daniel Bell's post-industrial society concept (and the elaborations by his adherents) was the pointed totalizing and deterministic foundations of the idea. For it is now apparent that Americans were facing a crisis of confidence in the early 1970s and were eager to grasp a techno- logical quick fix for the social, economic, and political problems facing the coun- try at that time (Siegel & Markoff, 1985).

Despite his disclaimers to the contrary, Bell clearly gave his readers the impression that "a new social framework" driven by computers and telecommu- nications would dramatically alter "the way in which economic and social exchanges are conducted, the way knowledge is created and retrieved, and the character of the occupations and work in which men engage" (1980a, p. 501). As he put it, as late as 1987, the "third technological revolution—the joining of com- puters and telecommunications"—will usher in a revolutionary age that he refers to as the "wired nation" (1987, pp. 10–11). He bluntly concludes that the "new technology" constitutes "a set of changes that pervade all aspects of society and reorganize all older relationships" (1989, p. 166).

In this way Bell attributes the post-industrial society to a technological devel- opment—the computer. As Mark Poster (1990) points out, in doing so Bell privi- leges intellectual technology as an "independent variable" in the post-industrial society, and indicates "that it determines other dependent variables, such as capi- tal and labor" (p. 24). The effect of this, Poster insists, is to leave the reader with a powerful explanatory equation:

computers + telecommunications = post-industrial society.

That equation "depicts the entire field of social reality as uniformly and homo- geneously affected by the introduction of computerized mass media" (p. 24). The implication, as Frederic Jameson (1991) points out, is to see technology as the "ultimately determining instance" of social and economic life (p. 37), and to ren- der the reader "powerless" in the face of this unstoppable force. The result for "people who have grown cynical or discouraged about other aspects of social life," says Langdon Winner (1986), is that they became "completely enthralled by the supposed redemptive qualities of computers and telecommunications" (p. 105). While we intend to delay our discussion of library literature until later in the book, it should be obvious to our readers that the most influential post-industrial enthusiast in our field, F. W. Lancaster, posited the same kind of totalizing and determinist formula: computers + telecommunications = paperless society (and the end of library history).

Given the extent and nature of the serious analysis of the role of technology in society, it should come as no surprise that the deterministic vision of the post- industrial society encountered instant and varied attention. Immediately, many students received Bell's vision with dark foreboding. Critics who viewed technol- ogy as a threat or curse were well armed with the arguments of a distinguished

European philosopher, Jacques Ellul. In *The Technological Society*, Ellul (1964) argued persuasively that Western technology, now operating according to its own inner logic, was clearly the dominant force in our society. Everywhere he looked Ellul saw "suicidal submission" to technology that was not so much planned as it was a result of the natural "laws of development" of technique.

Other critics with leftist inclinations drew equally ominous conclusions as they insisted that we must start our critique of Bell's vision "from the proposition that the social organization and operation of communication systems can properly be understood only by analyzing the structure of social inequality and the consequent differential access to key communication resources across the population" (Golding & Murdock, 1986, p. 71). For critics with this ideological tendency, the trouble with the post-industrial society is that it promises nothing more than what Brian Winston (1989) insists will be "business, and I mean business, as usual" (p. 72).

In short, critics of this persuasion (see Beniger, 1986) would insist that Bell's privileging of the computer as the "independent variable" in the post-industrial society is nothing more than at worst a deliberate, or at best misconceived, attempt to mask the fact that our era is better seen as "late capitalism," and that the post-industrial advocates have the "obvious ideological mission of demonstrating, to their own relief, that the new social formation in question no longer obeys the laws" of capitalism (Jameson, 1991, p. 3). This mistaken and wrongheaded privileging of the computer as the independent or "axial" principle of our society has rendered the metaphor so meaningless, says Fred Block (1990), that it has come to mean nothing more than "contemporary America" (p. 5). Carolyn Marvin (1987) concludes that "information age rhetoric is the start-fresh propaganda of our age" (p. 61).

Another major source of concern in the critical literature on the post-industrial society has been the conviction that the concept carries embedded within it not only the mistaken idea of autonomous technology, but also the controversial notion of neutral and benevolent technology (Bowers, 1988; Feenberg, 1991). Summarizing this view, David Nye (1990) argues that no technology is a neutral "implacable force moving through history," and he reminds us that rather "each technology is an extension of human lives: someone makes it, someone owns it, some oppose it, many use it, and all interpret it" (p. ix). Langdon Winner (1977) demonstrates at length that the "notion that technical forms are merely neutral . . . is a myth that no longer merits the least respect" (p. 325). One of the most forceful critics of neutral technology was the German existential philosopher Martin Heidegger (1977, p. 4), who concluded that technology was indeed a powerful force that had to be *actively* contended with:

> Everywhere, we remain unfree and chained to technology, whether we passionately affirm or deny it. But we are delivered over to it in the worst possible way when we regard it as something neutral.

The history of technology reveals, Carolyn Marvin (1988) points out, that the studies framed exclusively within an "instrument-centered" model overlook the fact the development of technology "is less the evolution of technical efficiencies in communication than a series of arenas for negotiating issues crucial to the conduct of social life; among them, who is inside and outside, who may speak, who may not, and who has authority and may be believed" (p. 4). Marvin further argues that the focus of the study of technology must be "shifted from the instrument to the drama in which existing groups perpetually negotiate power, authority, representation, and knowledge" (p. 5).

Numerous other students of technology support this view (Feenberg, 1991; Feenberg, 1995; Feenberg & Hannay, 1995), and insist that "the blithe claim that the apparatus, techniques, and organized systems of this modern age are merely neutral" is naive, dangerous, and unfounded (Winner, 1977, p. 279). All insist that each new technological development is a "social construction," that the terms of its adoption and influence will be socially determined, and that those who act on the idea that technologies are at once autonomous, neutral, and benevolent are destined to encounter dramatic and contradictory results (Bijker, Hughes, & Pinch, 1987; Bijker & Law, 1992; Layton, 1986; Nye, 1990). Carla Hesse (1996, p. 29) concurs when she reminds us that the information revolution has focused our attention on a range of previously "transparent choices;" namely: "how we determine . . . to use these information technologies and toward what ends."

We would do well to remember that technologies frequently find their origins in deliberate *intent*. Jennifer Slack (1984) counsels that it is vital to abandon the idea of neutral technology and encourages us to conceptualize technologies as "both causes and effects that are integrally related to the environment" (p. 146). To abandon action and passively accept predetermined technological outcomes would be to render ourselves at the mercy of "autonomous" and "neutral" technology. With courage and understanding, William Mitchell (1995, p. 5) insists, "we can concieve and explore alternative futures, we can find opportunities to intervene, sometimes to resist, to organize, to legislate, to plan, and to design."

THE TECHNOCRATIC VISION AND ITS CRITICS

While many of Bell's critics were troubled by his technological determinism, they were equally disturbed by the elitist and technocratic underpinnings of his work. Numerous scholars have noticed the strong links between Daniel Bell's ideas and the proposals put forward nearly 200 years ago by the French sociologist Henri, Comte de Saint-Simon (Badham, 1984; Frankel, 1987; Liebowitz, 1985). Saint-Simon was among the first to glimpse the emergence of the new industrial society, "the iron age," and to suggest forcefully the concomitant rise of a new elite of scientists and technicians who would bring a unique rationality and intellectual morality to bear on the management of society (Kumar, 1978).

When Bell's full-blown theory of post-industrial society was published in 1973, many reviewers noticed the technocratic emphasis in his work. For instance, George Ross (1974) commented that Bell desires "rule by the princes of technocracy," while Trent Schroyer (1974) concluded that post-industrialism "represents the most sophisticated type of technocratic theory." Victor Ferkiss (1979) argued that Bell aspires to a "rationalized, planned society run by technicians ... one in which systems analysis will essentially replace politics" (all quoted and cited in Robins & Webster, 1987, p. 105). Alvin Gouldner (1979) forcefully concludes that "the Platonic Complex, the dream of the philosopher-king with which Western philosophy begins, is the deepest wish-fulfilling fantasy of the New Class" (p. 65).

Bell's technocratic vision is explicit in his privileging of the new "intellectual technology" and "theoretical knowledge" as the "axial principle" of the post-industrial society. Since the emerging class of information professionals or "knowledge elites" will naturally consist of those most capable of applying theoretical knowledge and intellectual technologies effectively to the ever more complex problems faced by post-industrial societies, they are singled out for a special destiny in the information society. One of the key passages supporting this conclusion is found in Bell's (1973a, pp. 343–344) insistence that

> In the post-industrial society, what is crucial is not just a shift from property or political criteria to knowledge as the base of new power, but a change in the *character* of knowledge itself. What has now become decisive for society is the new centrality of *theoretical* knowledge . . .
>
> If the dominant figures of the past hundred years have been the entrepreneur, the businessman, and the industrial executive, the 'new men' are the scientists, the mathematicians, the economists, and the engineers of the new intellectual technology.

"In the post-industrial society," Bell continues, "production and business decisions will be subordinated to, or will derive from, other forces in society" (p. 344). Those other forces in society will be the new class of information professionals: "not only the best talents but eventually the entire complex of prestige and status will be rooted in the intellectual and scientific communities" (pp. 344–345). As Rienhard Bendix notes (1974), "this passage and many others like it read *as if* Professor Bell was reviving the technocratic visions of the 1920s" (p. 101).

Andrew Ross (1989, p. 225) nicely summarizes the post-industrial conception of the role of the information professionals when he notes that the "knowledge elite" was seen in purely "functional" terms:

> In their version of the new class as a functional elite risen to power in the transition from a production-oriented economy to a postindustrial service economy, the primacy of theoretical knowledge is seen as both *just* and *justified*. Just, because a trained technical elite ought to be more rational in its management of power than a

hereditary elite, and justified, not only because it distributes more evenly the share of access to power, but also because it simply promotes efficiency.

Ross concludes that "postindustrialists like Bell tend to describe the new technocratic class as a simple response to the benign needs of capitalism" (p. 225). Robins and Webster (1987) confirm this reading when they point out that Bell's forecast of the rise of a new knowledge elite is justified on "technicist grounds." "It is because of the 'exponential' growth of knowledge and the multiplications of fields and interests," they note, that "the concentration and centralization of social knowledge—with all its *political* implications—is explained on the basis of *technical-administrative* criteria" (p. 101).

This technological elitism has been the source of widespread uneasiness among Bell's critics, not the least of whom have been leaders in library and information science. While Chapter 4 addresses this matter in some detail, it nevertheless is necessary here to highlight some of the most pointed objections to Bell's position. First, we can identify those critics who would insist that the idea of a "knowledge elite" represents nothing more than a clumsy attempt on the part of the professional middle class designed to protect "the guild privileges secured by cultural capital" in the 21st century workplace (Ehrenreich, 1989; Ross, 1989, p. 226). Or, as Lawrence Veysey (1982) pointedly remarks, Bell's book gains much of its appeal as an "in-group manifesto" directed at likeminded knowledge workers who will find his embrace of the elite control of society of considerable appeal (p. 59). As a headline in *Info World* (November, 1990) gleefully put it: "Knowledge Keepers Will Rule in 21st Century." The idea that information professionals will be more powerful than "captains of industry" has become a powerful "intellectual smack," notes Timothy Luke (1989), one that "remains a narcotic delusion of incredible proportions" (p. 252).

Bell, of course, insisted that one vital characteristic of the new era would be the emergence of a true "meritocracy" where intelligence and advanced education would dictate individual life chances. He also noted that this new meritocratic approach to the distribution of rewards would surely prove very controversial. How controversial became obvious with the publication, in 1994, of *The Bell Curve* by Richard J. Herrnstein and Charles Murray, which bluntly predicted the rise of a "new cognitive elite," and went further than Bell in naming the winners and losers in the new information economy. It was the explicit naming of winners and losers that generated a vertible firestorm of argument and opened the authors to charges of racism and sexism (Fraser, 1995; Jacoby & Glauberman, 1995). But students of Bell's work noted that it was inevitable that someone would come along and push his ideas on post-industrial technocracy to their logical extreme (M. H. Harris, 1996).

A second, and clearly relevant, critique cynically dismisses the post-industrial society and its "knowledge elite" as one more clever, but transparent, attempt to convince American consumers to buy, buy, buy (Noble, 1984). Theodore Roszak

(1986) sharply criticizes "academicians as well as academic experts" for irresponsibly endorsing the post-industrial hype, and the result, he insists, is that society is "awash with commercially motivated exaggerations and the opportunistic mystifications of the computer science establishment" (p. 45). James W. Carey (1989) agrees and pulls no punches when he alleges that "the promotion of an illusion of an 'electronic revolution' borders on complicity by intellectuals in the myth-making of the electrical complex itself" (p. 138).

More intense, and carrying with it troubling political implications, is the claim that Bell's "knowledge elites" constitute nothing more than the old antidemocratic elites in new clothing. These critics, many of whom are librarians, remain skeptical of the very idea of a "neutral" technical elite and rebel at the notion that the problems of the age require elite and centralized control of the political decision-making process. Technocratic solutions to the problems of increasingly large and complex societies have a long history running from Saint-Simon, to Ortega y Gasset, Thorsten Veblen, and Edward Bernays, who conceived of the idea of the "engineering of consent" and public relations; to Edmund Wilson, who called on his fellow intellectuals in 1932 to "become engineers of ideas;" to Daniel Bell who sees the emerging information professions as a just, and justified, "meritocracy." As Andrew Ross (1989) points out, these technocratic discourses "assume the technobureaucratic process of rationalization as a benign and necessary fact, invoking its virtues for the 'soft' science of persuasion through the 'hard' metaphor of engineering" (p. 260, nt. 28).

However, the benign and neutral role of technocrats has always been intensely contested, with special attention being focused on the antidemocratic foundations of the technocratic ethos. Almost 100 years ago the Russian philosopher Mikhail Bakunin put the case against technocracy in this way:

> the reign of *scientific intelligence* [is] . . . the most aristocratic, despotic, arrogant and elitist of all regimes. There will be a new class, a new hierarchy of real and counterfeit scientists and scholars, and the world will be divided into a minority ruling in the name of knowledge, and an immense ignorant majority. And then, woe unto the mass of the ignorant ones. (quoted in Derber, Schwartz, & Magrass, 1990, p. 5)

Critics from left (Webster & Robins, 1986) to right (Bruce-Briggs, 1979) have carefully scrutinized this matter, and most have concluded that Bell's vision of a new technocratic meritocracy carries hidden within it "a representational shorthand for grasping a network of power and control even more difficult for our minds and imaginations to grasp" (Jameson, 1991, p. 38).

Many claim to see a political power play hidden beneath the surface of the new technocracy and fear the further erosion of citizen participation in public decision making. Richard Fox (1982) bluntly concludes that Bell's work represents just another "society with a new legitimation for elite control" (p. 74). "The cult of expertise and professionalism," Edward Said (1983) points out, "has so restricted our scope of vision" that a "positive doctrine of non-interference" has taken hold. The underlying logic, according to Said, is the belief that "the general public is best left ignorant, and the most crucial policy questions affecting human existence are best left to 'experts'" (p.136; Pacey, 1983; Winner, 1977). The post-industrial society is, thus, according to its critics, a "grand political gesture" (Segal, 1985), a rhetorical gambit, or, as Jacques Ellul (1990) put it, a daring and dangerous "technological bluff," which represents an "ideological call for born-again unity" (Marvin, 1987) in a world rigidly controlled by a "new class" of technocrats who hold a "notion of *citizenship*, which consists in serving one's own function well and not meddling with the mechanism" (Winner, 1977, p. 207). The technocratic mentality assumes that most members of the society lack the expertise or credentials necessary to participate in the management of the post-industrial society, and that the people should defer to expert leadership in this inegalitarian but just social order (Sosa & Harris, 1991). Critics of this view counsel resistance to the rise of the "new mandarin order" (Derber, Schwartz, & Magrass, 1990).

Daniel Bell, of course, has not been silent in the face of these challenges. In his pivotal essay on "The Social Framework of the Information Society" (1980a, p. 543), he strikes out at his leftist critics:

> the fear that a knowledge elite could become the technocratic rulers of the society is quite far-fetched and expresses more an ideological thrust by radical groups against the growing influence of technical personnel in decision making.

Against his right wing critics who claim that the "new class" will reflect the adversary culture characteristic of 1960s America, Bell (1979) soothingly replies that the new class notion is a "muddled concept" of little use in explaining developments in the information society and that it is clear that the new class will not be "its master." "In seeking to map the course of social change," Bell insists, "one should not mistake the froth for the deeper currents that carry it along" (p. 189). Chapter 4 of this book keeps Bell's dismissal at arm's length while considering, in detail, the problems and potential associated with the rise of the information professionals in the post-industrial society.

Before we leave the debate swirling around the technocratic vision of the post-industrial society, we must briefly examine one more issue that has garnered considerable attention. The problem lies in the technocratic understanding of the "policy-maker-as-rational-actor" model, which (implicitly at least) proceeds on the assumption that there exist no fundamental conflicts of interest, and that once research has clarified the possible consequences of a policy decision, "conflicts will vanish," or, at least in theory, we will see an "'objectively correct' policy" (Coleman, 1982, p. 168). Margaret Archer (1990) insists that this kind of "techno-rationality" or "instrumental reason" tends to relegate all "socio-political problems to the status of technical questions for which technical solutions would be forthcoming" (p. 102).

Archer sees this attitude as the first signs of the emergence of what she calls the "Fallacy of Amoral Objectivity" wherein the "high-tech hopefuls" project a world where "the cultural realm becomes subordinate to information technology" and technocrats, and where "there is no other basis than the instrumental rationality which it fosters on which to criticize it, evaluate it, decide how to deploy it or when to restrict it" (p. 109). This approach, she argues, "makes ethics superfluous" and promotes "moral agnosticism"(p. 111). She concludes that post-industrial theorists have a tendency to conflate "instrumental rationality with morality and technical advance with social progress" and that this disposition leads them to overlook completely the fact that we cannot address the question of what is rational without first deciding what is "best" (p. 117). This conflation of instrumental rationality with morality leaves many students of Bell's work with fears for the ethical future of society (M. H. Harris, 1986b; Johnson, 1984; Mitcham, 1986; Winner, 1977).

THE COMMODIFICATION OF INFORMATION AND ITS CRITICS

"Why," asks James Beniger (1986), "has information, among the multitude of commodities, come to dominate economic statistics" and "why the growing importance of microprocessors and computers, devices that can do nothing more than convert information from one form to another" (p. 31)? These questions stated in so many places and in so many ways remain two of the most troubling, and controversial, aspects of the information society debate. As Carolyn Marvin (1987) notes, the "question is how the commodification of information has come to be regarded as an empirically and theoretically correct representation" of economic and cultural activity in the information society (pp. 57-58). Whatever the answer to that question, she notes that we appear to be developing an increasingly "ethnocentric and historically provincial" conception of information that narrows its definition to "forms of expression and transaction in which it becomes a self-contained series of autonomous products without context" (p. 57). The result, unsatisfying to Marvin, is that we seem to view "real" information as that which is "divisible into quantities of printed letters or electronic bits," as a commodity for sale on markets, and as a "definite quantity increasing daily in determinable amounts . . . all *important* information is digital" (pp. 57, 59).

The discussion of this contemporary debate can delay us only briefly here, but we will return to this subject in most of the following chapters. For now it is appropriate to note that the controversy relative to the commodification of information in the post-industrial society represents one of the most contested aspects of the metaphor, and in many ways that facet is most heavily freighted with ideological baggage. At this juncture we only intend to highlight the contours of the debate by first attempting to answer the question posed above, and then turning to just two of the "eccentric angles" of critique of the idea of information as a commodity—or *the* commodity—in post-industrial society.

In beginning to answer Beniger's question relative to the emergence of information as the commodity, one must begin with the work of Fritz Machlup (1962, 1980, 1982, 1984) and that of Marc Porat (1977, 1978). Machlup was one of the first to perceive the emergence of something called the "knowledge industry," and he was clearly the most painstaking student of the question of the definition of "knowledge production." Porat was primarily concerned with the measurement of the size of the "information economy," and his work provided the trend lines so extensively drawn upon by Bell and other information society enthusiasts (Riedinger, 1989).

Students of Bell's work will remember that this deployment of demographic statistics on employment drawn from Porat's studies leads him to conclude that over half of the American workforce was engaged in "information work" and that information or "theoretical knowledge" had become the essential commodity in the post-industrial world. It was this, to Bell at least, unmistakable trend that led him to deduce that we were witnessing a "changeover from a goods-producing society to an information or knowledge society" (1973a, p. 487). These same trends led Bell to propose a new theory of value, "the knowledge theory of value," which he claims explains more about the information society than Marx's famous, but now obsolete, "labor" theory of value. Thus, Bell himself clearly points at the emergence of information as *the commodity*; that is, to "divine a new pattern of the production, distribution and consumption of information as the chief attribute of the new epoch" (Poster, 1990, p. 26).

Perhaps the largest firestorm of debate about the information society was generated by the *political* implications of the commodification of information for the future of a democratic society. Numerous students of liberal democracy have concluded that a principle feature of all such models is the notion that the success of the experiment always depends on the widespread and enlightened participation of the citizenry in the political decision-making process. As a corollary, liberals have always insisted that the widespread and equitable access to information was a key to the successful operation of a democracy (Dahlgren, 1987; Shapiro, 1986). That is, "information" is viewed as a "public good" and access to information should be "free" and unobstructed.

Mark Poster (1990, p. 27) sharply highlights the position of the critics of the commodification of information when he notes that

> It is something of a scandal that a major liberal thinker of the twentieth century, like Bell, should reverse this principle. Just when the merger of mass communications and the computer makes possible the rapid, universal distribution of information,

and therefore in principle extends radically the democratization of knowledge . . .
Bell sees fit to authorize the restriction of information to those who can foot the bill.

In this way, Poster notes, Bell "lends legitimacy to the extension of the commodity form to the new realm of information" and, thus, undermines the longstanding liberal principle that "in a democracy, knowledge and information in general must be freely accessible" (p. 27). The prominent sociologist Irving Horowitz (1991) finds Poster's argument absurd, insisting that it denies the reality that "knowledge is a hard-earned value" and has never been "free" and that such a "presumption . . . is as groundless as the notion of original goodness" (p. 9; see also Friedman, 1979). Horowitz decries the current and unproductive "dichotomization" between the information-as-commodity camp and the "free use" camp, and hopes for a quick and constructive resolution of the debate.

Nevertheless, the post-industrial emphasis on "informationalization" (Luke, 1989) or the "industrialization" of information (Herron, 1988), or the "mercantilization" of information (Lyotard, 1984) has driven many to conclude, especially within the library profession, that what we are witnessing is a subtle (but dangerous) attack on democratic values (Birdsall, 1994; Brook & Boal, 1995; H. Schiller, 1996). As Golding and Murdock (1986) argue, "the picture that emerges . . . is of a thriving electronic market place in which prevailing patterns of consumer detriment—the compounded disadvantages of low-income groups—are being replicated as new communications and information services come on line" (pp. 81-82). Harold Fromm (1991, p. 251) notes the changing nature of information access when he concludes that

> The marketplace of ideas, once only a metaphor, has literally become just that, a system of commodities. The Information Society . . . is an exchange of ideas that is largely an Exchange of Ideas (as in "Chicago Mercantile Exchange"), where information commands a price and is traded like pork-belly futures.

Many others are convinced that the amplified tension between the First Amendment conception of information as a "public" good and the notion of information as a commodity available only at a price can only contribute to expanding the gap between the information rich and information poor, and to a further erosion of democratic participation in the policymaking process (Wresch, 1996). As Everett Rogers (1986) coolly concludes after a thorough literature review, "if the forces of free competition are allowed to operate unfettered by public policies, access to the new communication technologies will usually be unequal" (p. 170).

Of course, not all share this concern. An equally large camp of conservative and liberal to radical theorists insist that the combination of computers and telecommunication technology promise a renaissance in democratic participation as the extent and availability of information is dramatically enhanced in the information society. Langdon Winner (1986, p. 103), who remains skeptical, summarizes this view as follows:

> Widespread access to computers will produce a society more democratic, egalitarian, and richly diverse than any previously known. Because "knowledge is power," because electronic information will spread knowledge into every corner of world society, political influence will be much more widely shared.

In our own literature F. W. Lancaster (Lancaster, Drasgow & Marks, 1980, p. 188) addressed the critics of information-as-commodity with the following confident dismissal:

> It is true, as it has always been, that the wealthier organizations and individuals can afford to purchase a higher level of subject expertise or a more rapid response in information services, but virtually no citizen of the United States is deprived of access to needed information through inability to pay for it. Fortunately, the electronic networks developed in the past twenty years have not created an information elite but have improved access to information for all segments of society.

Perhaps it is enough to say at this point that the critics of the "pay-per" society (Mosco, 1989) remain unconvinced, and they continue to insist that we must resist the idea that communication technologies be devoted totally or in the main to the profit motive (Slack, 1984, p. 146).

Another critique of the commodification of information pivots around the tendency of post-industrial enthusiasts to conflate the ideas of "information" and "knowledge." This group of critics is frankly puzzled by the idea that the speedy production and dissemination of information can be equated with the creation of knowledge (Midgely, 1989; Nunberg, 1996; Wolfe, 1993). They caution us to beware of heady "discursive cocktails" that equate an "information society" with an "informed society." They raise, without resolving, a series of questions that have troubled many in library and information science. For instance, they contend that information and knowledge are distinct *layers* of understanding, and that the simple suggestion that more information translates unproblematically into knowledge runs counter to the findings of 50 years of research in cognitive psychology. Most would insist that knowledge is "paradigmatic" and that information is meaningless without conceptual schemes designed to allow for the integration of information. As Jan Ekecrantz (1987) notes, the value of information has "less to do with its objective content than with its potential instrumentality" to the knowledge frames and social interactions of each individual (p. 88).

These critics notice that the conflation of knowledge with information, or the "identification of information with meaning" (Woodward, 1980), assumes that all that is necessary is more information. This troubling assumption contributes to what Langdon Winner (1986) calls "mythinformation," that is, the assumption that "speed conquers quantity" leads people to conclude that "the efficient management of information is revealed as the *telos* of modern society, its greatest mission" (p. 115). Critics note that this ideology of "mythinformation" completely overlooks the problems associated with "information overload" (Klapp, 1978), and ignores the fact that there "is not a scrap of evidence that our capacity to absorb information has markedly changed because of this monstrous regiment of data . . . nor that the regular provision of 'facts' beyond our limited capacity to absorb them materially alters our ability to run our lives and societies" (Winston, 1986, p. 367).

Even Daniel Bell (1985) himself has recently entered the debate by criticizing the tendency, so evident among post-industrial enthusiasts, of endorsing the notion that information and knowledge are one and the same. He rejects such reductionist logic and notes that too many writers confuse "information with knowledge, and the two are not the same" (p. 17).

Thus, we must conclude that the post-industrial society formula that suggests that the exponential growth of information governed by computers and rapidly disseminated by telecommunications technology will effortlessly translate into the equation of information = knowledge = progress leaves many serious students unconvinced.

ELECTRONIC WRITING AND
THE END OF THE BOOK REVISITED:
DISPLACEMENT THEORIES AND THEIR CRITICS

Before leaving our consideration of the various "angles of vision" detectable in the critical literature on the post-industrial or information society we must briefly attend to one further concern, a concern that has generated an inordinate and peculiarly emotional response among library and "book" interests. This concern is prompted by some extremely loose and exuberant talk about the power of the computer to create a "paperless society" and dictate the end of the "book." Once again it is Daniel Bell (1980a) who appears to have widely publicized this notion when he casually noted that the combination of computers with telecommunications technology promised the "reduction if not the elimination of paper in transactions and exchanges" and the concomitant marginalization of the research library to the status of a "sad monument of the printed past" (pp. 529, 533). F. Warren McFarlan (1984, p. 100-101) saw the solution as a simple matter of efficiency:

> No example is more striking than the situation confronting libraries. They have a 1,000-year-plus tradition of storing books made of parchment and wood pulp. Soaring materials costs, the advent of cheap microfiche and microfilm, expansion of computer data bases, and electronic links between libraries will make the research facility of the year 2000 unrecognizable from the large library of today. Those

libraries that persist in spending 65% of their budget to keep aged wood pulp warm (and cool) will be irrelevant to the needs of their readers.

This reductionist notion was eagerly endorsed by countless writers, especially in library and information science, and aggressively attacked by the friends of the book. Among the most excited endorsements of the idea came from the pen of F. W. Lancaster who repeatedly concluded (despite an occasional touch on the brake pedal) that "as print on paper publications give way and are eventually completely replaced by electronic publications" all libraries other than "archival repositories of the printed records . . . are likely to disappear" (1982a, p. 150). Without books, libraries will become "crumbling institutions" with little or no "future." "We are moving," he noted, "rather rapidly and quite inevitably toward a paperless society" (1978a, p. 356).

James Thompson (1982) took this argument to its ultimate reductionist and determinist conclusion when he wrote in *The End of Libraries* that the computer represents a "pre-emptive technology," which he predicts "in due time will displace the larger part of mankind's present book-centered communal memory" (p. 13). Drawing on a now-popular analogy, Thompson insists that "in evolutionary terms the obvious analogy is with the spectacularly sudden extinction of the dinosaurs" (p. 16). As one unrepentant determinist put it, "the library is becoming disembodied, disappearing, like the Cheshire Cat" (Molholt, 1988, p. 37). All such predictions focus on or around the year 2000 as a particularly popular moment for the "end of the book," the "extinction" of the book-centered library, and the division of the library profession into two classes: the new class of information professionals and the marginalized "undertakers" of a lifeless form of communication.

As Jon Theim (1979) points out in a brilliant essay entitled "The Great Library of Alexandria Burnt," it has long been the case that many *learned* antagonists of letters have celebrated the burning of the Great Alexandrian Library because such a destructive act gave fresh license to the creative spirit unburdened by the accumulated weight of historical memory. What contemporary librarians find particularly provocative about the current celebration of the destruction of our modern Alexandrian libraries is the degree to which this celebration confronts the idea of great repositories of books with intense hostility.

Aimed as they were at the library and book community, these displacement theories were clearly designed to garner attention and provoke discussion. Unfortunately, their effect was to polarize the field, and, thus, much of the discussion and dialogue in the literature has taken the form of equally reductionist defenses of the book, which only distract the participants in the argument from the real issues in the matter. Everywhere we turn, we find what James Carey (1984) calls episodes "in nostalgia" wherein friends of the book rise to its defense just at "the moment we are about to lose it" (p. 105; see D. Lacy, 1982). Carey argues that these "neo-Luddite" symbolic book crusades are only "the simplistic obverse of the mythos of the electronics" (1989, p. 139).

Perhaps the most forceful recent example of this "simplistic obverse of the mythos of the electronics" would be librarian Michael Gorman's (1994) remarkable essay entitled "The Treason of the Learned." In that essay Gorman soberly suggests that a massive "antilibrary, antibook" conspiracy is afoot in America (Harris & Hannah, 1996). Gorman howled that this conspiracy was being managed by "technovandals" who intended nothing less than the destruction of the "print-based knowledge and information industries." And then Gorman aggressively accuses all who are so foolish as to embrace the new information technology as coconspirators, or even as traitors! An equally passionate, and admittedly "Luddite," defense of books and reading is found in Sven Birkerts (1994) *Gutenberg Elegies* wherein the author forsees the end of our cultural heritage in a flurry of disconnected bits and bytes. These Luditte defenses—more or less hysterical—of the book are appearing (and disappearing) with dramatic speed as we move more rapidly toward the moment when digital communication becomes the dominant communication medium of our era.

The reason that we insist that this drift in the discussion of the future of the library is so unproductive is that displacement theories have always proven to be untenable, and more importantly, because the empirical evidence on the status of the book *proves* that displacement theories explain very little about recent history (Manguel, 1996; Martin, 1994). Virtually all serious students of the history of communications technology note that new "writing technologies" never relegate older technologies to the "dustbins" of history. "People did not stop talking when they learned to write," Ithiel de Sola Pool (1982, p. 25) notes, "and they did not abandon pens when the typewriter came along." Henry Petroski (1990) reinforces this view when he notes the failure of displacement theories to explain the fact that 14 billion pencils were manufactured in 1989 (see also Czitrom, 1982; Graff, 1987; Pattison, 1982).

As far as books in libraries go, one might consider the following simple facts. In 1970, when the idea of the death of the book first emerged, we witnessed the publication of some 35,000 new "book" titles, and in 1984 that figure had grown to 50,000 with another 100,000 titles being imported that year (Epstein, 1990; Handlin, 1987). Further, the electronic journal in many fields seems rather slow in arriving. In 1988, some 5,000 new journals in print form were established, bringing the total to something over 110,000 titles, while the number of electronic journals could be counted on one hand (Peek & Burstyn, 1991, p. 101). While many (Lancaster, 1995; Peek & Newby, 1996) continue to believe that e-journals will replace the printed scholarly journal sometime in the future, the book appears to be alive and well and rumors of its demise appear to be greatly exaggerated. Bell (1985) himself dismissed the suggestion that books would be replaced by "electronic writing," and even the generally unrepentant F. W. Lancaster (1985) noted that his ideas had not "achieved universal acceptance" and that it was now apparent that "the replacement of print on paper is not inevitable" (p. 555). Thus, while displacement theories must be simply dismissed as mistaken, or viewed as rhetorical gambits designed to provoke heated debate, it does not follow that one can simply disregard the significance of "electronic writing" for the future of communication and libraries (Bloch & Hesse, 1995; Nunberg, 1996).

Two much more serious concerns must be briefly considered. First, we must examine the evidence that supports the claim that the privileging of science and "theoretical knowledge" in the post-industrial era promises a decline or further marginalization of the "humanistic" in thought and practice, and a decline in our ability to think critically. Second, we must attend to the troubling and challenging evidence that suggests that the emergence of new writing technologies have the potential for literally changing the way in which we *think*.

As regards the first issue, many people have noticed that the information society privileges science and scientific knowledge in a way that marginalizes certain kinds of critical thought felt to be vital to Western civilizations. With "the hegemony of computers," Jean-Francis Lyotard (1984) points out, "comes a certain logic, and therefore a certain set of prescriptions determining which statements are accepted as 'knowledge' statements." He concludes that we are witnessing a shift in the valorization of the "use value" of knowledge (pp. 4-5). Ben Agger (1989) has labeled this shift as "fast capitalism" and insists that we are experiencing a time when a "purely technical reason" is "reducing intellectual judgements to matters of sheer utility," and thus undermining "the possibility of critique's utopian imagination, desperately needed today" (pp. 54, 3). Timothy Luke (1989) concurs, arguing that "informationalism's" privileging of "cybernetic-electronic technics" has generated a "complex new order whose social and political structures are dominated increasingly by the development, elaboration, and expression of formalized discourses and scientific disciplines" (p. 10). The result, Luke concludes, is that these "changing codes of substantive values and knowledge have come to define meaning, generate power, and frame the choices of everyday life" (p. 10).

Margaret Archer (1990) argues that we must not acquiesce in this "shift," for "if the whole cultural realm becomes subordinate" to this "techno-rationality" the realm of ethics and critique will be rendered "superfluous" and we will have no ground other than "instrumental rationality" from which to view and evaluate the new science (p. 109). William Irwin Thompson (1989) also notices this development and refers to it as the "deconstruction" of the text, where "difference," speed, and economic use define value. The Pulitzer Prize-winning historian Daniel Boorstin (1982) labels this as the age of the "imperial instant-everywhere" and calls for renewed attention to the significance of knowledge in the context of the "whole everywhere-past" that is critically scrutinized in the precious search for "finding order and meaning in the whole of human experience" (pp. 1386-1388). The "informatization" of social life, the librarian John Swan (1988) insists, must be viewed as a serious threat to critical consciousness, and reflexive efforts must be made to counter the "decontextualization and the disembodiment" of our understanding of the world so that we may plan our future in the context of "the whole fabric of memory and knowledge" (p. 28). Yet others, such as Paul Levinson (1989), insist that "text in electronic environments amenable to instant and universal access, infinite connection and reference, modifiability and interactivity, is an ideal vehicle for expression" and for the development of active and critical minds (p. 396). Nevertheless, we contend that the concern expressed by these commentators represents a much more relevant and meaningful context for discussion than the simple computer versus book theme so prevalent in our literature.

Finally, we must reflect on the intensely contested view that new "writing technologies" literally change the way in which we think. While empirical evidence is thin, and while our conclusions must be viewed as extremely tentative, it does appear as if there is some reason to believe that computers and electronic writing might actually alter the "human psyche." Many students of this matter begin with Walter Ong's (1967, 1982, 1986) idea of "transformative writing technologies" that Michael Heim (1987) defines as a "historical shift in the symbolization of reality" and that, according to Ong and Heim, bring with them "a restructuring of the psyche . . . . the entire human personality is configured anew with every shift in the dominant medium for preserving thought" (Heim, 1987, p. 59). The question of interest here, argues Joshua Meyrowitz (1985), is "why and how do technologies that merely create new connections among people and places lead to any fundamental shift in the structure of society or in social behavior" (p. 23)? "The change involves more than the adaption of language to new material conditions," the literary historian Cecelia Tichi (1987) insists, for "behind the shift of images are new, technological definitions of the human relation to the world" (p. xii).

One of the most provocative responses to this question is found in the work of Mark Poster (1990). He asserts that we are entering an "electronic stage" of communication that represents a whole new "mode of information" that will alter the "configuration of information" or what he calls the "wrapping of language" (p. 8). Poster insists that communication has become an "autonomous realm of experience" in our current "mode of information" and that we are witnessing the emergence of new "language formations that alter significantly the network of social relations, that restructure those relations and the subjects they constitute" (p. 8). He concludes that we are observing the beginnings of a societal "paradigm shift" wherein the "solid institutional routines that have characterized modern society for some two hundred years are being shaken by the earthquake of electronically mediated communication and recomposed into new routines whose outlines are as yet by no means clear" (p. 14). And other scholars like Allucquere Rosanne Stone (1995) argue persuasively that communication theories modeled on face-to-face exchanges must be dramatically revised when we deal with computer-mediated communication (e.g., e-mail) that allow individuals to "invent" and "reinvent" themselves at will (Barglow, 1994; Wittig, 1994).

We can, perhaps, glimpse a hint of what the future holds by confronting the new digital hypertext systems. As George Landow (1992, pp. 2–3) noted

> Many . . . who write on hypertext or literary theory, argue that we must abandon conceptual systems founded upon the ideas of center, margin, heirarchy, and linearity and replace them with ones of multilinearity, nodes, links, and networks. Almost all parties to this paradigm shift, which marks a revolution in human thought, see electronic writing as a direct response to the strengths and weaknesses of the printed book.

Landow and others (Bolter, 1991; Barrett, 1992; Heim, 1993; Landow, 1994; Lanham, 1993) are persuaded that hypertext will represent the means by which we learn first to read differently, and then, it is believed, to think differently. Jay David Bolter (1991, pp. 2–3) insists that while "the shift from print to the computer does not mean the end of literacy," it does mean the end of the "literacy of print":

> The computer is restructuring our current economy of writing. It is changing the cultural status of writing as well as the method of producing books. It is changing the relationship of the author to the text and of both author and text to the reader.

If such changes prove in time to be real, it is indeed possible that hypertext might spark new ways of *thinking* (Turkle, 1995). What appears clear is that we should view with skepticism the casual suggestion that the shift from print to electronic writing represents nothing more than a simple change in "format."

INTERLUDE: THE POPULARIZATION OF THE "POST-INDUSTRIAL" METAPHOR AND THE ADOPTION OF THE INFORMATION SOCIETY

We are nearing the end of our discussion of the post-industrial society construct and the outlines of the debate that Daniel Bell's powerful metaphor elicited in American society. Before concluding this chapter, it is necessary to consider briefly the reasons for the apparent success of Bell's vision in both predicting and molding the "future." As we noted earlier, part of the reason for his success has to be situated in the uncommon ability of the "astute social theorist" to state his vision in ways that would at once appear to offer solutions to major problems facing a society gripped by "severe self doubt" while at the same time offering a reasoned explanation that, despite its contradictions and faults, appeared to resonate with the experience of vast numbers of people.

Writing in the 1960s and 1970s, Bell timed his vision of a "way out" beautifully, and Americans eagerly embraced his prophecy of a "fresh start" that would not only eliminate our ills but propel the United States to unheard of heights of economic prosperity and social development. This conclusion is confirmed by the extent to which the general public, and many of the post-industrial enthusiasts, overlooked the dark and brooding aspects of Bell's analysis in order to emphasize the positive. The process was essentially complete with the publication of two enormously popular glosses on Bell in the form of the work of John Naisbitt (1982) and Alvin Toffler (1980) and the selection of the computer as "Man of the Year" by *Time* magazine in 1982.

Another major source of Bell's success surely lies in his subtle privileging of the new class of "information professionals" as the heroes of the information age. This idea had irresistible appeal to intellectuals, businessmen, government officials, teachers, librarians, and all others who immediately recognized the potential for personal growth in status and wealth in the new information society. These powerful allies tended to endorse Bell's metaphor uncritically and proved invaluable in spreading his vision to every corner of American life.

But these partial explanations for the success of Bell's metaphor should not be expected to carry too much weight. For clearly he was on to something real, and whether or not he was correct in labeling the development of the post-industrial society a "revolution," he clearly glimpsed a significant change in the way in which "economic and social exchanges are conducted, the way knowledge is created and retrieved, and the character of the occupations and work in which men engage" (1980a, p. 501). This sense of change dictated by computers and telecommunications technology was most readily apparent in corporate America. Recent studies have confirmed Bell's vision in a surprising number of particulars. As the report of the distinguished *Management in the 1990s Research Program* at the Massachusetts Institute of Technology (Allen & Morton, 1994; Morton, 1991) concluded, information technology broadly defined is the key new component in corporate America and it is changing "the way people work, the way society's major organizations are structured, and the way corporations will collaborate and compete in the years to come" (Morton, 1991, p. v).

This same report (Morton, 1991) offers significant confirmation to Bell's prediction that information would replace goods as the key commodity in the American economy, and notes the extent to which "today's world capital markets could not exist without information technologies" (p. v). The "deconstruction" of the global monetary system with its "fixed values of exchange," argues William Thompson (1989), demanded an information technology that could capitalize on the new reality that "*difference* became the source of wealth." A powerful new industry built on the new social framework of computers plus telecommunications technology, and focusing on "information" as a commodity, sprang forth to deal with a marketplace "expanded to planetary scale" where fortunes are made or lost in global transactions "contracted to seconds" (p. 9).

Finally, we must remark on the extent to which Bell's vision became a "generative metaphor" (Schon, 1979) that was capable of stimulating and guiding powerful social forces that, in part at least, created an environment in which the information society could become a self-fulfilling prophecy. We intend to return to this matter in Chapter 3, but for now we need to emphasize the extent to which the information society project, as expressed by Bell and his adherents, was a rhetorical gambit and designed to *persuade* (Nelson, Megill, & McCloskey, 1987). "The effort at persuasion introduces a nice circularity into the process," William Leiss (1989) points out, for "if we can be cajoled into believing that some future state is inevitable, and further to alter our behavior in order to conform to its anticipated requirements, the end result will be a retrospective proof of the prediction's accuracy" (p. 284). Thus, it is now clear that Bell's vision proved extremely persuasive to Americans of all walks of life, but especially to government and corporate leadership, school administrators and teachers, university administrators and faculty, leaders in the communications industry, librarians, and other pivotal opinion leaders who devised and implemented policy initiatives that have gone a long way toward changing social behavior, and, thus, "confirming the model's predictions about what was 'inevitable'" (p. 284).

CONCLUSION: INTO THE INFORMATION SOCIETY

We do not consider this book as a sort of historical "afterthought"—an analysis of the post-industrial society after the party is over. Certainly, Bell's critics have scored many points in the contest to prove or disprove the idea that the post-industrial metaphor explains developments in contemporary America. We should not let, however, the obvious shortcomings of Bell's vision blind us to "the significant developments in new technology, with their accompanying occupation changes and general shifts in the whole gamut of socio-political relations" (Frankel, 1987, p. 2). Instead, it seems apparent that something very real is happening to contemporary society as a result of the emergence of information technology, the commodification of information, and the rise of the new class of information professionals. Yet, we remain uncertain as to what it is (Kling, 1995; Tapscott, 1996).

We are increasingly convinced that Kimon Valaskakis (1982) is correct in suggesting that we must begin to think of the age in terms of (an admittedly awkward term) "informediation," which he defines as "the process by which an increasing number of human activities in *all fields* . . . are being either *mediated* or taken over by *high technology information machines*" (pp. 23–24). If we accept this new reality, we must also accept its "essential bias" that posits the "creation of new social formations tied to the exchange-driven production, distribution, consumption, interpretation and reproduction of information" (Luke, 1989, p. 11). J. David Bolter (1984) more elegantly refers to the computer as a "defining technology" and argues persuasively for his claim that information technology promises (or threatens) to alter a whole range of fundamental relationships in our society. He hastens to point out that he is not a technological determinist, but also insists that while "defining technologies" seldom do away with their predecessors "entirely," they nevertheless have the power to gain dominance in the technological realm and powerfully influence every other aspect of socio-political life (p. 8).

While it seems undeniable that we are dealing with a new "social framework" in Bell's sense, it also appears clear that we must find some way to transcend the two most common reactions to the information society—"the complacent (yet delerious) camp-following celebration" or the "moralizing condemnation" so common to our literature (Jameson, 1991, p. 46). In short, we must find a way to confront critically and intervene intelligently in the process of change sweeping our society and, more explicitly, our profession.

One promising way to engage in this project of critical intervention is to acknowledge the extent to which the information society is an "ideological construct" designed to create as well as describe the future. We must not lose sight of the fact that post-industrial theorizing is part of an "epic tradition." As Howard Segal (1985) points out, this form of theorizing is "not separate from practice but rather is itself a form of practice," and the "action that it seeks is the realization of theory . . . precisely 'to make the world reflect a theory'" (p. 160). "The deconstruction of the social definition of the information revolution," Kees Brants (1989) reminds us, "means tracing a process of interaction between technological advance as a reality, the reacting and defining actors and a wider ideological environment which is culturally and historically grounded" (p. 81).

The following pages intend to attempt to avoid the "instrument centered" technological determinism so characteristic of our literature, and, instead, follow Carolyn Marvin's (1988) suggestion that the problem is "less the evolution of technical efficiencies in communication than a series of arenas for negotiating issues crucial to the conduct of social life" (p. 4–5). It now appears time to undertake a critical and systematic examination of the promise and the significant social risks of the information society. To do so we must acknowledge the extent to which the "information age" is part of a "complex social formation," and accept the difficult task of dissecting the "specific effective relationships between those technologies and the social formation in order to critically evaluate those relationships and propose strategies for intervention" (Slack, 1984, p. 146). James Boyle (1996, p. ix–x) makes the point even more forcefully when he notes that

> Right now, behind the visible information revolution in technology and economy, a significant but unexamined process of rhetorical and interpretive construction is going on. This process of construction produces justifications, ideologies, and property regimes rather than mainframes. . . . Yet it will shape our world as thoroughly as any technical change. To understand this process, one needs more than a modem or multimedia kit; one needs a social theory of the information society.

2

Librarians Confront the Post-Industrial Era

Every gain in knowledge and efficiency and every outworn symbol or causal explanation displaced by more realistic analysis, is potentially a gain in ease and richness of living. But when this new knowledge is not put to work in the service of all the people, when it is only partially applied to those able to "pay for it" or bright enough to learn it unaided, or when it is used by those with power in order to exploit others, this knowledge may be either largely barren or, worse, it tends to become a disruptive factor.

Robert Lynd

The arguments for pay libraries may be made in the name of economic theory, efficiency, or inevitable economic trends, but in essence it is a political idea, just as the concepts of free public library service or free public education are political ideas.

Richard DeGennaro

THE MISSION OF LIBRARIES IN INDUSTRIAL AMERICA

Since the inception of the idea of a "library" in the United States, and more significantly, since the middle of the 19th century, librarians and the friends of libraries have been debating the proper role of the library profession. Initially, most librarians, and virtually all of the supporters of libraries, insisted that the professional role of the librarian, not unlike that of doctors and teachers, was to prescribe for their clients. In the librarian's case, of course, the cure was to come in the form of the deployment of a carefully selected army of books that would contribute to the amelioration of the ills of mankind (M. H. Harris, 1986a; 1995).

The literature of American librarianship is heavily freighted with articles insisting that the foundations of professional authority are to be found in the librarian's unique mandate to prescribe the kinds of books that people should read; at least if they choose to read books in libraries. The influential Melvil Dewey made this point unequivocally when he insisted in 1876, that the responsible professional librarian would select books so authoritatively, push them so vigorously, and reinforce their virtuous messages so steadfastly, that in time the librarian would come to control the "thought of his whole community" (Vann, 1978, p. 70). Such power, Dewey insisted, could be confidently placed in the hands of the professional librarian because of the library profession's well known, and selfless, commitment to the production and reproduction of a civically virtuous citizenry in the United States (Wiegand, 1996).

Thus, for most librarians the foundations of professional authority rested firmly on the library profession's mission as responsible censors of the reading material made available through the nation's libraries. However, in the first three decades of the 20th century, discordant voices began to be heard, and increasingly librarians were questioning the idea that they should operate as authoritarian censors of the public's reading. By the mid-1930s the debate had grown intense, and a new definition of the foundations of professional authority was rapidly emerging. The victory of the forces of reform was nearly complete with the adoption of the Library Bill of Rights in 1939 (Geller, 1984; M. H. Harris, 1976; Stielow, 1983).

Libraries were now portrayed as "arsenals of democratic culture," and the librarian was simply the neutral and passive conduit through which the day's intelligence would be transmitted to enlightened citizens in a democratic republic. The idea was to facilitate the democratic process by providing access to the whole spectrum of human knowledge, no matter how trivial or controversial, without consideration of its possible effects. The reader was to be given the authority to decide what information to use and how to utilize it.

The librarian was now mandated to take a neutral and passive position on all issues, and was expected to provide ample information on all sides of the issue in order to enable the user to make an informed decision. Pierce Butler (1933, p. 105) made the point, contra Dewey, with vigor:

> The library is no mission station for the promulgation of an established literary gospel that is eternally true. The librarian's duty is not to entice men, against their wills if need be, to convert themselves to his way of thinking. He is merely society's custodian of its cultural archives.

While this new view of the role of the library in American society quickly appeared to gain wide support, especially among the increasingly powerful intellectual freedom establishment of the American Library Association, many librarians remained skeptical. How, they wondered, could librarians ever hope to gain professional status if they functioned in a purely "custodial" role? How, they wondered, could librarians ever hope to become truly professional if the library was always privileged over the librarian in the new philosophy? And, how, they wondered, could the extreme relativity, passivity, and neutrality of the "new librarian" ever be considered as a suitable foundation for professional authority? Despite the valiant efforts of intellectual freedom advocates like David Berninghausen, the questions just would not die, and, in 1973, the troubled consensus was thrown into turmoil by the appearance of Daniel Bell's *The Coming of Post-Industrial Society*.

THE LIBRARIAN AS "INFORMATION PROFESSIONAL"

"Since the publication of Daniel Bell's *The Coming of Post Industrial Society* in 1973," Pauline Wilson (1978) noted, "'post-industrial society' has become a common phrase." She points to the initial appeal of Bell's book when she notices that "librarians have usually understood it to mean an enlarged role for information and knowledge, and by extension an enlarged role in society for their profession" (p. 124). Librarians, it would seem, were not immune to what Timothy Luke (1989) has referred to as the "narcotic delusion" that in the post-industrial era information professionals will be more powerful than the captains of industry, and that the post-industrial society will trail in its wake a new class of information professionals who will offer expert and authoritative advice to an information-hungry clientele. While Bell's vision of the role of the information professionals offered an unmistakable foundation for professional authority for American librarians, and the potential empowerment of the library profession, it also presented a clear challenge to the definition of "librarian" and "library" as they were embodied in the official credo of the American Library Association.

Elite members of the library profession seem to have encountered, and fully assimilated Bell's work by the mid-1970s, and in the latter part of that decade the library profession was swept by a wave, soon to become a tidal wave, of literature designed to alert professional librarians to the promise and pitfalls of the emergent post-industrial era. As early as 1977 the American Library Association was devoting its full attention to the post-industrial society (Josey, 1978), and a wide range of books and essays were produced with the purpose of helping librarians understand the implications of the emerging information society (Estabrook, 1977; Giuliano, 1978; Hammer, 1976).

In the past decade we have seen the idea of the post-industrial society employed with increasing frequency and intensity, and one of our principle purposes in this chapter is to attempt a cognitive mapping of the emerging politics of the post-industrial society as reflected in the complex constellation of texts addressing the question for the library and information science community. At first glance it is immediately apparent that the idea of the post-industrial, or information, age has been viewed by library and information professionals in the same contradictory fashion that it has been viewed by the intellectual community in general. For some librarians, the metaphor has decidedly positive connotations, while for others it connotes a dangerous and threatening future. For many, post-industrialism represents a unique opportunity to transcend the structural and functional constraints that have for so long inhibited our desire to achieve genuine professional status. For others, post-industrialism promises nothing but cultural decline. As we critically examine this literature we quickly note the rapidity with which the metaphor has amassed a host of usages, and the extent to which the idea of the "post-industrial" has become, at once, a rallying cry for those who seek a dramatic break with our past; a heuristic device designed to help us understand the "new era" or simply "the object of desire, signifying a state of being 'with it' at any price" (Hoesterey, 1991, p. ix). The task of sorting out this babel of voices is daunting, but it is a project that must be undertaken if we are to address critically and systematically the implications of the post-industrial era for library and information services (for one very useful recent attempt see Kling & Lamb, 1996).

Perhaps the best place to begin is to note that this period witnessed the appearance of a powerful and aggressive new voice, one that argued that librarians should capitalize on the emerging information technology to resolve long-standing management problems and at the same time place themselves at the very forefront of the new information professions. Indeed, it was probably inevitable that the library profession should find its own version of Daniel Bell within its own ranks, and that discovery was soon in coming with the emergence of F. W. Lancaster as the most outspoken and influential advocate of the librarian as "information professional."

F. W. LANCASTER, THE "PAPERLESS LIBRARY," AND THE LIBRARIAN AS INFORMATION PROFESSIONAL

Frederick Wilfrid (F. W.) Lancaster was born in Durham, England, in 1933. After training in the School of Librarianship at Newcastle upon Tyne, he ultimately became a Fellow of the Library Association of Great Britain. After holding a series of responsible positions in Great Britain, Lancaster moved to the United States where he worked as a special librarian and as an Information Systems Specialist at the National Library of Medicine. In 1970, he joined the faculty of the Graduate School of Library and Information Science at the University of Illinois.

Lancaster was fully conversant with Daniel Bell's work, and clearly excited by the possibilities inherent in Bell's vision of the post-industrial era. Lancaster had

increasingly come to view the book-as-artifact as a major constraint on the refor-
mation of American library service, and he excitedly endorsed Bell's vision of the
information age and its implications for library and information services in the
United States. For Bell's casual suggestion that the computer combined with telecommunications technology and expert systems would render print-on-paper
communication obsolete was music to Lancaster's ears. He, perhaps more than
any other librarian, saw the revolutionary potential of the new technology, and his
keen intellect and clear writing style were quickly brought into play in the effort
to persuade librarians that the new technology should be embraced as emancipatory. His determination, and his astute translation of Bell's vision for librarians,
have elevated him to the status of the profession's foremost advocate of the
"paperless library" and far and away the most widely read and cited author in our
field (Hayes, 1983; Budd & Seavey, 1996).

The initial stimulus for this published onslaught on the library profession was
apparently provided by a grant awarded by the National Science Foundation to the
Library Research Center at the University of Illinois Graduate School of Library
Science in 1978. The purpose of the grant was to underwrite the preparation of a
report on the effect of the "paperless society" on "what libraries and librarians
may be doing in 2001" (Lancaster, Drasgow, & Marks, 1980, pp. 162, 167). This
study provided the foundation for everything that Lancaster wrote about the role
of libraries and librarians in the "paperless society," and it is this study, in its two
principal incarnations, to which we must now turn our attention.

As we do so we cannot help but notice the parallels between Lancaster and
Bell. Lancaster, like Bell, tends to pepper his works with contradictions, and he
shares Bell's tendency to declare his work a "fiction," or a "scenario" while alter-
nately suggesting that what he is describing is reality, or at least the inevitable outcome of the forces at work in American society. Lancaster, like Bell, is prone to
"sprinkling" his essays with qualifications while at the same time always arriving
at conclusions that appear to suggest that his totalizing vision is "privileged" and
explains the process of change for all libraries in the United States. Finally, Lancaster, like Bell, aggressively portrays the "paperless society" in technocratic
terms, and repeatedly gives one the impression that he is a technological determinist. All of these and other similarities between the two theorists will be discussed later, but for now we must turn to a systematic analysis of Lancaster's
totalizing vision of a "paperless society."

The National Science Foundation (NSF) study that constitutes the foundation
for all of Lancaster's published work on the "paperless library" was designed to
examine the "effects on libraries and librarians of the predicted transition from a
print-on-paper to a paperless society" (Lancaster, Drasgow, & Marks, 1980, p.
167). The investigators point out that they proceeded in a three-step process:

- A detailed review of the relevant literature;
- A Delphi study; and

■ The development of a scenario to depict what libraries and librarians may be doing in 2001.

After this preliminary work the scenario was submitted to the Deans of Accredited Library Schools and to 50 percent of the Directors of the Association of College and Research Libraries (ACRL). Then, the scenario was read and discussed by the participants at the 1979 Clinic on Library Applications of Data Processing at Illinois, and was subsequently published in the professional periodical *Collection Management*, "with a request for input from the profession at large." It was the final version of this "scenario" published repeatedly in essay and book form, and in a variety of "registers," that sparked one of the most intense debates in the history of American librarianship. In order to understand this controversy, and to assess the impact of the post-industrial society on library and information services, we must undertake the difficult task of deconstructing the complex janus like history of "the scenario."

While this task is extremely complicated, a fruitful beginning can be made by noting the assumptions underlying the scenario. "The basic premise underlying our ongoing research," Lancaster points out, "is that many types of publications can be distributed more effectively in electronic form and that, in fact, future economic factors will dictate that they be distributed electronically" (Lancaster, Drasgow, & Marks, 1980, p. 162). This premise, which has proven to be flawed, suggests that a form of economic determinism will rule the production and distribution of knowledge and information in society, and, as a result, the authors conclude that "clearly, we are evolving out of this paper-based era into one that is electronic" (p. 162).

The reasons for this inevitable evolution from paper to electronic writing are clear: (1) the information explosion, (2) the dramatic increases in the costs of the print-on-paper distribution system, and (3) the "general inefficiency" of the current system (p. 163). All of these factors have caused a "decline in accessibility" that must continue "as long as we continue to print, publish and distribute in the same way we have been for the last 300 years" (p. 164). Thus, the steady decline in the efficiency of the print-on-paper system in conjunction with the escalating costs of the distribution system demand a change to electronic systems. Predicting the future is risky business, and Lancaster's work is full of penetrating judgments mixed with a good deal of nonsense. These failings will be the subject of our concern later in this chapter, but for now we must simply describe the scenario that "predicts" the future for libraries.

"Looking back from the vantage point of this, the first year of the twenty-first century," Lancaster notes, "it is clear that the library profession has not escaped the upheaval that has beset all segments of society in the past twenty-five years" (Lancaster, Drasgow, & Marks, 1980, p. 168). Most notable in the changes affecting libraries has been "the rapid decline of the *artifact*—particularly the printed book—as the primary device for storage and transmittal of recorded knowledge, and the replacement of these artifacts with *data* . . . virtually all of these data now being accessible electronically" (p. 170). Also significant has been the "deinstitutionalization" of the library profession, and the emergence of the information profession which offers vastly increased status and opportunity for the "information specialists" who were capable of capitalizing on the entrepreneurial opportunities "outside the traditional library setting" (p. 170). The fate of those unable or unwilling to adapt to this new environment goes without comment.

Now we can see the fundamentals of the "paperless society." The computer combined with telecommunications technology and expert systems will *displace* the print-on-paper system and, thus, render both traditional libraries and librarians obsolete. Forward looking and opportunistic "information specialists," however, will thrive in the "paperless society" by moving from the public sector "custodial" function to a private sector "entrepreneurial" role.

Now as an "exercise" in "scenario writing" Lancaster's work represents an interesting and provocative contribution to the discussion of the implications of the post-industrial era for libraries, and as such is harmless enough. However, Lancaster (like Bell) has a tendency to deploy his scenario in a register in which the definition of one variable becomes the depiction of the whole society. In this way Lancaster is "doing something to the reader" and astutely transforms his "scenario" into a privileged explanatory framework for the interpretation of the future of the library.

The controversy surrounding Lancaster's metaphor can only be understood in the context of this subtle metamorphosis of his scenario into a unerring vision of the future of libraries, and the best way to see this process at work is to examine what is perhaps the most cited and commented upon essay in the history of modern librarianship. In a paper entitled "Whither Libraries? or, Wither Libraries?" Lancaster (1978a) dropped his cautious approach and moved aggressively to persuade librarians that the paperless society was not only inevitable, but good. The change in register is evident in the "Conclusion" to that paper which begins with the statement "we are moving rather rapidly and quite inevitably toward a paperless society" (p. 356). In this sentence we see the often commented upon substitution of totalizing absolutes for the more cautious "scenario" approach utilized in the original NSF study. Now we read that the end of the print-on-paper system is "*inevitable*," and that while at present books exist this situation will "*undoubtedly*" change, and we will "achieve *completely* paperless systems" (italics added, p. 356). His mission becomes clear when he insists that "the profession seems to have its head in the sand" and that unless we move aggressively to position ourselves advantageously in the paperless society we may not survive (p. 357).

In a flurry of papers in the same register Lancaster hammered away at his theme, and all of these papers are characterized by a tendency toward more dogmatic, determinist, reductionist, and technocratic visions. In each paper the theme is the same. First, there is the bad news: In the paperless society "the library as an institution will begin its inevitable decline" (1982a, p. 151). Then, there is the good news: "The librarian of the electronic age could become a valued professional" and this "could greatly improve the librarian's image, status and (dare we hope?) rate of compensation" (p. 154).

Or, as he put it differently in 1983, "I see little future for the library" but "the librarian could long outlive the library" (p. 750). But, only if librarians abandon their obsession with the custodial preservation of the book-as-artifact and become "electronic librarians." By all indications the future was bright (Lancaster, 1982a, p. 150):

> Librarians need no longer operate within the four walls of an institution. They can apply their professional skills in searching information sources and in answering questions wherever they can plug in a terminal. They can freelance from the home or form themselves into group practices as doctors and attorneys do. These trends, of course, are already quite evident in the profession.

As Lancaster became more persuaded by his own rhetoric, his totalizing vision grew more breathless. For instance, when thinking about what librarians would be doing in the year 2001, he notes that the "major professional tasks" carried out by librarians in the paperful library were selection, cataloging, and reference work. But in the "electronic world" all of these tasks will become obsolete, and since no one need come to a library the electronic librarian must move outside of this "crumbling institution." Book selection, cataloging and classification, and traditional reference work will all become irrelevant, and even management skills will become unnecessary for "after all there may not be many libraries around to be managed" (Lancaster, 1983, p. 753). Of course, all of this will happen by the turn of the century.

Such statements reflect the dangers of totalizing visions, and the peculiar dangers associated with visioning the computer as an independent variable in society (thus, paperless society) while at the same time considering all other variables as dependent upon this new technology. This led Lancaster to suggest that the production and use of knowledge in American society are dictated by the *format* in which knowledge is distributed. The emergence of the computer and telecommunications technology would dictate an end to one mode of scholarly production and initiate another, and as an aside, spell the end of libraries.

Chapter 1 spelled out the problems with such technological determinism, and one need only remark here that, in privileging the computer in this way, Lancaster misunderstood the political economy of scholarly production. In his emphasis on the economic benefits of electronic writing he failed to notice that the current political economy of scholarly publishing and (not perishing) operates within a context that is full of economic contradictions (Carrigan, 1990, 1991; M. H. Harris, 1991). This is one of the most apparent reasons why we have seen developments in publishing-in-paper-form (and in libraries) that disprove Lancaster's scenario in nearly every particular. Derek Bok (1986), formerly President of Harvard University, once noted that "published research" is the "common currency of academic achievement, a currency that can be weighed and evaluated across institutional and even national boundaries." He further notes that the publication of research in prestige journals and monographs is the means "by which communities confer status and establish hierarchy" (p. 77).

Thus, scholars are reluctant to experiment with new channels for publication like electronic journals. Peek and Burstyn (1991, p. 113) concisely explain the situation when they note that

> the tendency will be for scholars to publish through traditional channels first, because the status of traditional journals is understood by those responsible for promotion and tenure decisions. Electronic journals, unless add-ons to print, will most likely be considered only by those established scholars who wish to experiment or by those who are unsuccessful in publishing their work elsewhere.

And while a number of e-journals are now available, and while librarians and others continue to suggest that it is simply a matter of time before we move into the era of the e-journal, progress has been glacial to this point (Lancaster, 1995; Peek & Newby, 1996). Carol Tenopir (1995) summarizes a number of studies (Schauder, 1994; Shamp, 1992) that demonstrate the degree to which scholars are still avoiding e-journals.

All those who harbor fantasies of the ability of librarians to control the *production* of knowledge might benefit from reflection on William Shepherd Dix's simple reminder that librarians neither produce nor consume knowledge, they only collect, preserve, and transmit it. "When scholars are ready to package the results of their labors in some form totally different from the printed book, and the consumers want this form," Dix noted, "the librarian will do what he can to facilitate the transfer" (Harris & Tourjee, 1983, p. 70). We might hope, but could hardly expect, that librarians will wield much power over the production and distribution of knowledge anytime in the immediate future.

Another significant cause for the failure of Lancaster's model to prove of real value in predicting the future of libraries was his apparent misunderstanding of the organizational culture of American librarianship. In privileging scientific "data," in his inability to think of information as anything other than a commodity to be sold on markets, and in his casual dismissal of professional activities (selection and cataloging) central to the operation of libraries, Lancaster overlooked the library profession's intense commitment to the idea that "knowledge" must be viewed as a public good that is made readily and equitably available to all citizens in a democratic society. Like Bell, Lancaster succumbed to the determinist vision that implies that machines will dictate changes for the whole society, and that people have no choice but to ride the wave or drown in a "paperless society." While the logic of his argument was indeed powerful, it simply overlooked the fact that people will and must intervene in the implementation of new technologies, and that these "interventions" will control the direction and pace of organizational change.

Lancaster finally came to this realization in 1985 when he "revisited" his famous essay. He suggested that his rather naive idea that "just as the printed book replaced earlier written forms of communication, it could and would itself give way to something else" had proven to be incorrect, and he concluded that "the replacement of print on paper is not inevitable" (Lancaster, 1985, pp. 554, 555). Noting that his determinist metaphor had failed to recognize that the impact of a new technology "is determined by the qualities of the humans who exploit it, rather than by properties inherent in the technology itself," Lancaster remained unable to understand the reasons for the library professions' reluctance to embrace his vision (p. 555). "As far as I have been able to tell," Lancaster notes, "rejection of electronic publishing is more often than not based on the rather vague feeling that the printed book is an indispensable element in our society and that it has been with us too long to be easily displaced" (p. 554). Still unable to see the controversy as anything other than a Luddite resistance to progress he concludes that "this argument, of course, is complete nonsense" (p. 554). And finally, for Lancaster's latest reflections on technology and libraries see his "Has Technology Failed Us?" (1991a, pp. 12–13), in which he concludes "let us not delude ourselves into believing that it has had a substantial impact in improving the services that a library provides to its users, that it has greatly improved the image of the librarian, or that technology alone will increase the perceived value of library and librarian in the future."

Our assessment of the predictive power of Lancaster's metaphor should not be interpreted as a condemnation of his vision, nor should we be interpreted as suggesting that he was completely mistaken. Clearly, he recognized: (1) the potential of the computer to propel libraries into an era of enhanced efficiency and usefulness, and (2) the structural and functional restraints imposed on the library by its symbiotic relationship with the high culture book industry in America. In this sense his work represents a progressive vision that could legitimately be referred to as emancipatory, but unfortunately the register of his discourse framed the debate in a extremely reductionist and unconstructive way. As Svend Larsen (1988) noted, Lancaster's presentation of his metaphor tended to narrow the debate to emotional arguments about "whether the library and the printed word will have any raison d'etre in a society based on information technology" (p. 159). As a result, the early reception of Lancaster's metaphor reflected a polemical contest that focused almost exclusively on the *format* of the materials in libraries. This distracting sideshow has tended to misdirect the dialogue from fundamental and vital questions to matters of little consequence, and has too often involved little more than exasperated and exasperating name calling.

The reasons for this myopia are, with hindsight, fairly clear. It is anchored in Lancaster's narrow and nearly exclusive use of library literature in the construction of his "scenario," and his privileging of the library in the construction of the "paperless society." While he was aware of Bell's work (e.g., Lancaster, 1980a), in the main he tended to read and cite the library literature on the paperless society. This "micro-sectoral" approach to the question lead to a kind of closure in Lancaster's consideration of the problems and potential inherent in the post-industrial era. Thus, while Lancaster carefully acknowledges the sources of his ideas for a "library without walls" (Taylor, 1975) and the "paperless library" (Licklider, 1965), he remains virtually oblivious to the much more important questions being debated in the interdisciplinary literature on the post-industrial society that are discussed in Chapter 1 of this book. This is why he appears so unaware of these issues in his "paperless society revisited" (Lancaster, 1985) and tends to misunderstand the controversy surrounding his vision of the paperless society.

Unfortunately, Lancaster's limited exploration of the critical literature on the post-industrial society had a even more serious effect. For since his work was so central to the library profession's consideration of the post-industrial era, it followed that his failure to address the larger issues (and literature) acted as a sort of force field that blocked access to the critical literature on the matter. Librarians are only now beginning to break out of the narrow frame imposed by Lancaster's pivotal studies, and to confront systematically the much expanded literature on the subject of the post-industrial society nearly 20 years after the parameters of the broader debate were being clearly discussed in the interdisciplinary context. This case study illustrates the pitfalls encountered by a profession that comes to believe that it can understand its world through an exclusive reliance on "library literature."

The result was the polarization of the library profession and the emergence of two diametrically opposed (and uncompromising) positions. The first, represented best by Daniel Boorstin (1982) insists that "the autonomous reader . . . is the be-all and end-all of our libraries" (p. 1388). "This argument, of course, is complete nonsense," the paperless library enthusiasts would reply, and they would sadly conclude that librarians are simply "soft on books" and should be disdainfully brushed aside as out of step with a future that the profession has no choice but to accept. Maurice B. Line (1981) noticed that this polarity of views had suppressed the vital question of "access" to knowledge and information and ignored the simple reality that, in certain contexts, some modes of communication serve this objective better than others.

This is not to suggest that there were not voices raised in an attempt to redirect the discussion to the more substantive issues. Indeed, authors repeatedly tried to alter the landscape upon which the debate was conducted, but to little avail. For instance, Blaise Cronin (1983) pointed to the ethereal nature of the debate, and worried over the extent to which "scenario spinning" was controlling the discussion. He chided both sides for their tendency to name-calling, "inflexibility," and "surprise-free" visions in an environment that was clearly unpredictable. He also cautioned librarians to beware the mistaken notion that technology constituted an "independent variable." He further remarked that the idea of a "radical break" in our history was unproductive, and calmly suggested that we should expect evolution, what he called "genetic drift," and not expect too much too soon (p. 280).

Line (1981) raised many of the same issues and noted that many of the disputants in the controversy "seem to me either naive or deliberately misleading" (p. 259). Richard DeGennaro (1985) commented upon the "fun and frustration" concomitant to the task of distinguishing the "pipe dreams from the prophetic visions" (p. 39). These isolated voices, however, were virtually drowned out by the noise and hubbub made by the two major camps in the war of words surrounding the intensely contested future of books and libraries.

Fortunately, this situation could not last forever, and slowly librarians have been turning their attention to more substantive questions relating to access to information in a democratic society. As a result, we can now turn to an exploration of the literature on these more substantive issues.

TECHNOLOGICAL DETERMINISM AND ITS CRITICS

We discussed the critical literature on technological determinism at some length in Chapter 1, but we must pause here for a moment to note the history of this idea in the debate on the paperless society. We have already commented upon the extent to which Lancaster deployed a determinist vision in his work. His insistence that the book would "inevitably" be replaced by electronic writing was a recurrent theme in his writings on the paperless society, and this was always linked to the notion that the future of libraries would be *dictated* by this technological development. Viewing this "natural evolution" in communication technology as neutral and benign Lancaster seriously underestimated the extent to which librarians would feel paralyzed in the face of this inevitable break with their historical roots.

Indeed, the early literature on the paperless society can be divided nicely into its "promise and curse" varieties. For those enthusiastic camp-followers who had viewed the library as anachronistic even before the emergence of the paperless society, Lancaster's vision offered a technological quick fix to all that ailed the library profession. These authors welcomed the arrival of the new "preemptive technology" and its destructive impact on the library "dinosaur" (Thompson, 1982). If the emergence of electronic writing spelled the end of the inefficient and wasteful library system it should be welcomed. Further, these enthusiasts euphorically and uncritically emphasized the fact that intelligent and opportunistic librarians could capitalize on the new environment in a dramatic fashion. Library literature was replete with this self-conscious but uncritical notion: while the paperless society is inevitable, we are well positioned to profit handsomely in the new era. This suggestion was always couched in terms that implied that librarians would not have to choose to do anything, but rather would be *forced to do some-*

thing, or at least, would find themselves in the position of doing something or becoming extinct (e.g., Campbell, 1993; Molholt, 1986, 1988; Park, 1992; Stoffle, Renaud, & Veldorf, 1996). "We're in an ideal win-win situation," American Library Association (ALA) President Richard Dougherty (1991) exclaimed, "our profession will become stronger, more valued, and better paid in the years ahead," while at the same time "admirably serving the larger national interest" (p. 182). For the celebrants of the paperless society it all seemed so "natural."

Those who uncritically accepted the deterministic vision but viewed the inevitable outcome as a curse went into immediate (and clearly premature) mourning for the book and the library. Asking whether there will be a role for librarians in the post-industrial society, Klaus Musmann (1978) sadly concludes that the librarians' traditional role as "transmitters rather than the originators of culture" will probably relegate the profession to the dustbin of history (p. 233). We find innumerable examples of what James Carey (1984, p. 105) has labeled exercises "in nostalgia" wherein bibliophiles gather to grieve for the book "at the moment when we are about to lose it" (see Gorman, 1994; McCook, 1993; Ring, 1996).

Fortunately, of late, librarians have become less taken with the determinist vision. More and more voices are being raised in critique of the idea of autonomous technology, and librarians (including F. W. Lancaster) appear to be much more alert to the fact that the uses and impacts of new technologies are largely social constructions (Berring, 1995; Budd, 1995–1996). While the hour is late, we at least appear to be emerging from our sleepwalk into a self-conscious awareness that the impact of the new technologies will be largely *determined* by librarians and other interested parties rather than the technologies *per se* (Buschman, 1993).

We need pause only briefly to document this point. In early 1990, ALA President Patricia Glass Schuman addressed the matter of "reclaiming our technological future." She insisted that librarians seemed to be emerging from the grips of the "paperless library fantasy" that leads us to assume that "the future will just happen, not that we can play a key role in inventing it" (p. 34). Noting that it was time the profession took hold of its future, Schuman suggests that we begin by recognizing that: "Our business is not information. Our mission is to facilitate understanding through knowledge" (p. 38). Shortly thereafter, John Buschman (1990) emphasized the same theme when he dismissed the idea that technology was autonomous and neutral. Insisting that librarians must begin at last to ask "the right questions about information technology," Buschman suggests a fundamental beginning: "Why is information technology good for libraries, librarians or the public?" (p. 1026). With this question as our guide, he suggests, we will be able to assess critically the "social and political consequences" of technologies and plan to intervene actively and self-consciously in the development of library and information services in the post-industrial era.

THE TECHNOCRATIC VISION AND THE LIBRARY
RESPONSE

We have already analyzed the technocratic underpinnings of the post-industrial vision as conceived of by Daniel Bell and his adherents. After briefly alluding to the technocratic focus of Lancaster's work, we must now explore this matter more thoroughly. In what is perhaps the best overview of the debate on the paperless library, or the "information paradigm," Richard Apostle and Boris Raymond (1986, p. 378) note that

> An aim of those who advance this information model is to convince librarians that they must abandon their old self perception as custodians of books and enter into the new world of information. For them the ideal information professionals are people whose work is focused on the processing of information, is frequently external to the library, is often freelance, who sell their services to a well defined segmented market and who are highly dependent on electronic technology . . . . One other important distinction is often emphasized: information workers get well-paid jobs, whereas librarians do not.

This theme, repeatedly stated, has, in the opinion of Apostle and Raymond, significantly impacted the "profession's self perception." Lancaster himself (1982a) most forcefully pressed this argument: "I expect to see the appearance of greatly increasing numbers of freelance librarians although, rather than working completely independently, they are perhaps more likely to form small group practices somewhat resembling present group practices in medicine and law" (p. 152). Insisting that librarians in traditional settings perform essentially clerical tasks, Lancaster argued that librarians in the paperless society "are likely to have responsibilities far beyond those they have at present," and indeed, this might require a name change for the profession (p. 152).

While Lancaster never offers a name for the new field, many others have. For instance, Pat Molholt (1986) likes the name "knowledge engineer" and sees the new profession as radically different from the old, and Patrick Wilson (1977) agrees, but likes the label "information doctor," while still others have embraced the idea of "cybrarians." Of course, the new information professionals will be dramatically empowered in the paperless society. William Moffett (1990, p. 97) nicely captured the sense of it all when he wrote

> A golden age of librarianship may be at hand. In post-industrial American society, the reasoning goes, a society in which access to information will be of paramount importance, in which educated and well-informed men and women will be one of our most important national assets, the role of those experts who mediate access to information will be an honored one. Librarians will no longer squat near the bottom of the academic totem pole.

In the paperless era information professionals will "mediate access to information" and provide expert solutions to problems vital to the society (Dowlin, 1980; Johnson, 1982; Veaner, 1985; Woodsworth et al., 1989). In the paperless era information professionals will be "proactive" and will "position" themselves advantageously for the future. Most importantly they will drop their passivity and deliberate sense of neutrality, for as Emily Fayen (1986, p. 241) stresses

> If librarians want to hold positions of authority in the future, they too must be prepared to take on the responsibility of providing real information and vouching for its correctness with their professional credentials.

"The information doctor aims," Patrick Wilson (1977) suggested, "at making prescriptions, at recommending effective techniques for attaining one's goals" (p. 118). Many librarians noticed the revolutionary nature of this new definition of the role of the librarian, and David Kronick (1982) cautioned that "before librarians say their final farewells to the book and to some of the cherished traditions of their profession, they need to look at the purposes, objectives, and goals to which they may also be saying their farewells" (p. 132). In the initial euphoria about the rosy future of librarians in the emergent information society most librarians ignored Kronick's cautionary note, and rushed headlong into an uncritical embrace of the "information paradigm." This early and uncritical acceptance of the "information paradigm" as a map to the profession's future led librarians to make increasingly authoritarian and technocratic proposals. One of the most vivid landmarks in this odyssey was the publication of the intensely contested *Mission Statement for Public Library Service* (Public Library Association, 1977). The extent to which the vision of the information professional as outlined by Daniel Bell, and the notion of the new role of the librarian as described by Lancaster, was being adopted by librarians is clearly evident in the key part of this document (p. 617):

> As a consequence of . . . information overload, the role of libraries for several thousand years, which emphasizes the preservation of the human record, has now become more complex, requiring hard decisions not only about what is to be preserved but also about what is to be discarded. Decisions are, and must, be made to erase portions of the record deemed to be insignificant, irrelevant, and unrepresentative, in order that the useful and pertinent be accessible. Society needs an agency to digest, evaluate, and make responsible decisions to retain or to erase the materials produced.

Policy statements, such as this, alerted the intellectual freedom wing within the American library profession that the new "information paradigm" constituted a serious threat to the cherished (and official) view of the library as a *neutral* and *passive* reflection of social intelligence readily accessible to all. The new "information paradigm" was a conscious challenge to the official position. Lancaster repeatedly notes that as the result of a "historical accident," the "library, rather than the librarian, has traditionally been the focus of our attention as a profession" (1983, p. 747). He correctly observes that "by focusing on the information professional as an expert in a technical field, rather than on an institution in which he or she operates, we could greatly improve the librarian's image, status, and (dare we hope?) rate of compensation" (1982a, p. 154). While this penetrating analysis of the reasons why librarians cannot be considered professionals is virtually unique to our literature, it also demonstrates Lancaster's failure to understand library history, for he overlooks the fact that the library was *deliberately* privileged by the profession in service of its mission to protect free and equitable access to information in a democratic republic.

At this point the most aggressive defenders of the library as "the arsenal of democratic society" moved forcefully into the fray, insisting that the technocratic vision of the information professional was a direct and dangerous challenge to the role of the library and the librarian as defined by the "Library Bill of Rights" and other official statements of purpose endorsed by ALA. One of the most sustained attacks on the "information paradigm" was launched by David Berninghausen (1979). Declaring that the advocates of the "information paradigm" seemed to be suggesting that "librarians claim the responsibility to repudiate the First Amendment by erasing or eliminating what librarians don't like," he insisted that librarians should never be allowed to "digest, evaluate, and make responsible decisions to retain or erase" (p. 13). "In our quest for status one of the first casualties is the lower class client," Leigh Estabrook (1981a) reminded librarians, and "the more we seek to establish our expertise, the more we become resistant to community control" (p. 126).

Lester Asheim, perhaps more than anyone else, made the most persuasive case against the "information paradigm" as a guide to the definition of the role of the librarian. In a pivotal essay entitled "Ortega Revisited," Asheim (1982) begins by noting that the debate over the mission of the librarian "takes on new and even more challenging implications in the light of current developments in library practices and new challenges to the library's social role" introduced by the advent of the post-industrial era (p. 215). Noting that the idea that the librarian should act as a filter or authoritative expert has definite appeal in the age of "information overload," he also recognizes that the librarian is seeking a firmer foundation for professional authority in the information society. He insists, however, that librarians must never consider themselves experts who would "prescribe" for clients, and he urges librarians to fight to avoid constructing a "mystique around our procedures that would require their dependence upon our intervention" (p. 223).

Indeed, in one of the most biting portions of his essay, Asheim warns librarians of the antidemocratic tendencies in the technocratic vision with its "arrogant assumption . . . that [experts] can define and eliminate, for everyone else, the 'useless' and 'stupid'" (p. 222). "Librarians," Asheim continues, "almost alone among the professionals, do not, in that sense, 'prescribe'" (p. 222). The role of the librarian must remain the neutral provision "of the largest possible store of information" so that the *user* can filter and evaluate that information without intervention on the part of the librarian.

After all, Asheim reminds his readers, the role of the *library* is to facilitate enlightened and active participation in the democratic process, and is, thus, political, and not economic. In this argument Asheim deliberately privileges the *library* and *the user*, while arguing that the passive and neutral librarian is vital to the effective reproduction of an enlightened citizenry in a democratic society.

This defense of the "traditional" role of the librarian is diametrically opposed to Lancaster's professional project. Asheim knows this, for as he notes elsewhere (1978), while the "role of the library in giving information *without prescription*" is a key attribute of the library in a democratic society, "this may keep us forever out of the traditional professional pantheon" (p. 253). He would appear to be correct, for there is nothing in the literature on the sociology of professions that would suggest that occupations can become professions while abrogating the responsibility of prescribing authoritative solutions to client-centered problems. Roma Harris (1993, pp. 874–875) supports this conclusion when she notes that historically the "relationship between client and librarian is much more centered on the client's need than it is on the librarian's role as expert." "The pursuit," she argues, "of the type of professionalism exhibited in the male fields is basically incompatible" with the traditional model of library service (see also R. Harris, 1992).

In rejecting Lancaster's definition of the mission of the librarian, Asheim and Harris tend to frustrate the professional aspirations of countless librarians. In doing so they highlight one of the most complex aspects of the "paperless library" construct. For while the idea appeals to status-starved professional librarians, it also clearly demands an abandonment of the librarian's cherished role as a neutral servant of democracy. If our democratic mission is privileged, then the librarian is forced to sacrifice his or her professional aspirations in the service of the higher goal (Sosa & M. H. Harris, 1991).

This contradiction highlights the confusion and frustration surrounding the debate on the role of the librarian in the post-industrial era. In many ways the disputants are speaking in different "registers." For the advocates of the information paradigm the question is essentially technical and economic. For the supporters of the librarian's role as outlined in the "Library Bill of Rights" the question is framed in essentially political terms. It is clear that the result has been the creation of a deep split between those librarians who insist that librarians must remain committed to neutrality and passivity even at the expense of professional status, and those who insist that librarians must move quickly and unequivocally to establish the foundations of professional authority within the context of the information paradigm. This debate will not end any time soon, and in many ways the rest of our book introduces the issues that the profession must consider in an attempt to define the mission of the librarian in the post-industrial era.

THE COMMODIFICATION OF INFORMATION, THE
INFORMATION INDUSTRY, AND INFORMATION
INEQUITIES IN AMERICAN SOCIETY

At this point we ask the reader to recall our discussion of Daniel Bell's post-indus-trial metaphor from Chapter 1, and his insistence that "information and knowl-edge," not "labor," are the crucial commodities in the post-industrial era. We have already noted the radical move made by Bell when he proposed to lend "legiti-macy to the extension of the commodity form to the new realm of information" as a result of his identification of "a new pattern of the production, distribution, and consumption of information as the chief attribute of the new epoch" (Poster, 1990, pp. 26–27). Librarians who have seen the information paradigm as the best guide to the future have adopted this notion, and have been aggressively suggesting that in the new age "information brokers" or "free lance librarians" will earn their liv-ing by selling information to the highest bidder. For such professionals the move toward the commodification of information represents just one more natural step in the extension of the efficiencies of the capitalist market system to the informa-tion services sector of the economy. Advocates of this new vision see the question purely in economic terms.

Anyone who reads the literature of library and information science knows that many, perhaps most, members of the library profession have seen it in quite dif-ferent terms. This latter group, conceiving of the question of the commodification of information within the context of the "Library Bill of Rights," argues that the question must be seen in political and cultural terms, and that librarians must resist (or at least cautiously approach) the commodification of information.

It is now apparent that this difference of opinion constitutes the most intensely contested aspect of the post-industrial metaphor as understood by librarians, and we must confront the various positions on this matter before we can effectively proceed to other questions. It is important to remember that the general consensus on the role of the library in a democratic society arrived at with the adoption of the "Library Bill of Rights" was formed in the context of Enlightenment beliefs about the role of an informed citizenry in a democratic society.

Numerous students of liberal conceptions of democracy have concluded that a principle feature of all such models is the notion that the success of the experiment always depends on the widespread, and enlightened, participation of the citizenry in the political decision-making process. As a corollary, liberals have always insisted that the widespread and equitable access to information was the key to the successful operation of a democracy (Brown, 1996; Dalhgren, 1987; Shapiro, 1986). ALA President Arthur Curley (1994, p. 691) rehearsed these themes when he wrote that all librarians believe that the "government has a constitutional duty to ensure that citizens are sufficiently well informed to make wise decisions," and that this duty is best fulfilled by providing "free and equal access to the widest range of information."

What troubles liberals most about Daniel Bell's post-industrial era and the con-comitant "commodification" or "mercantilization" of information is the appre-hension that this notion actually constitutes a systematic attempt to *restrict* access to information necessary to the successful operation of a democracy. Librarians have been quick to notice that commodification of information in the post-indus-trial era tends to amplify the tension between the conception of information as a "public good," and the notion of information as a commodity available only at a price. Many librarians fear that this tendency can only contribute to expanding the gap between the "information rich" and the "information poor," and contribute to the further erosion of citizen participation in the democratic process (Buschman, 1995; Givens, 1995). What is at stake for the liberal wing of the library commu-nity is Democracy itself.

F. W. Lancaster intensified this concern with his consistent inability to think of information (or "data") in anything other than economic terms. Despite an occa-sional qualification, he frequently links the paperless society to the commodifica-tion of information, and the end of libraries. He *implies* that librarians should abandon Article One of the "Library Bill of Rights." Lancaster's casual sugges-tion that ALA's official credo was rendered obsolete by the advent of the paper-less society can only be understood in the light of his tendency to view the whole question in strictly economic terms. What he failed to recognize was that his deterministic vision created a sense of urgency, but not quite in the way he had anticipated. His belief that the time for normative theorizing was over was undone by events, for as so often been the case, fears that social institutions face major challenges and that traditional professional practices are undergoing far-reaching changes produce a fertile hotbed for the intense examination of fundamental philosophical principles (Shapiro, 1990, p. 3).

Lancaster almost never seems to be able to see the political implications of his vision. On the few occasions when he does address the question, he does so in ways that suggest that he completely misunderstands the nature of the debate, and the intensity of the ideological firestorm that his work set off in the field. For instance, in one of the two places where Lancaster (Lancaster, Drasgow, & Marks, 1980, p. 188) addresses this matter he proceeds in the following manner:

> It is true, as it has always been, that the wealthier organizations and individuals can afford to purchase a higher level of subject expertise or a more rapid response in information services, but virtually no citizen of the United States is deprived of access to needed information through inability to pay for it. Fortunately, the elec-tronic networks developed in the past twenty years have not created an information elite but have improved access to information for all segments of society.

Sensing that this scenario might not set well with critics of the "pay-per" soci-ety, Lancaster (1980a, pp. 18–19) added a qualification in a second paper when he notes

The rapid spread of fee-based information consultants may cause a rift between "information rich" and "information poor." An "information elite," composed of those members of the community who can afford information services, may emerge. This situation could exist for a number of years while the "fee versus free" controversy rages throughout the profession. It will largely settle itself as costs decline and as public and academic libraries come to recognize that information service from electronic sources is as legitimate a service to provide to their communities and to subsidize as the provision of printed materials.

This casual suggestion that libraries will come to view "information service in electronic form" as a "public good" offers small consolation in the face of Lancaster's repeated insistence that libraries have no "future" in the paperless society, and that all librarians will eventually be working in libraries without walls as information brokers selling information-as-commodity on the free market. If the end of the library is "inevitable" what libraries will offer this subsidized service to the "information poor?" A careful reading of Lancaster's work on this subject would confirm the oft stated view that he is essentially indifferent to the "fee vs. free" controversy. Perhaps a better explanation would be that Lancaster shares Patrick Wilson's (1977, pp. 124–25) critical conclusion that

> It might appear that simply providing more documents to more people would be a means of equalizing the unequal distribution of knowledge . . . But the uneven distribution of knowledge in the adult population has causes that are entirely independent of the uneven availability of documents and too deep to be perceptibly influenced by a change in the conditions of availability of documents.

Librarians, intensely committed to the idea that the American library profession is an essential bulwark to democracy, could not remain indifferent to this question. Fay Blake (1978, p. 399) sounded the alarm for librarians when she pointed out that the widespread adoption of the information paradigm would expand the gap between the "information-rich" and the "information-poor" in American society. This sentiment has been repeatedly rehearsed in the professional literature and in the profession's official proclamations, and constitutes the most critical and sustained element in the attack on the "information paradigm" (Birdsall, 1994; Peters, 1995; Schement, 1996; H. Schiller, 1996).

Indeed, as Herbert and Anita Schiller noted in 1988, it is "accurate to claim that the commercialization of information is the transcendent question" in the debate about the role of the library in the post-industrial era (p. 154). Barbara Smith (1989) argues that librarians must abandon the deterministic theme underlying the information paradigm, and she insists that the "library's mission should drive its policy decisions" (p. 33). That mission has always been the idea of "Information Justice," Marilyn Gell (1979) suggests, and she argues contra Lancaster that "the specter of a caste system based on accessibility of information is a haunting and potent problem with which we must struggle" (p. 1736).

Brian Nielson (1989, p. 212) defines "Information Justice" as follows:

> For American librarianship, one key occupational value is the provision to the larger
> society of access to information in a barrier-free manner. Any inhibiting factor to
> information access, whether it is a poorly designed cataloging system, or a fee for
> admission, is thus negatively valued.

He insists that librarians must accept a fundamental change in the definition of
their mission if they come to see information as a "commodity." Anita Schiller
(1981) agrees and points out that librarians need to continue to insist that "social
criteria" and not economic concerns should govern the debate on the role of the
library in the future.

A great deal of support for the claim that librarians have come to see the commodification of information as antithetical to the "Library Bill of Rights" could be
deployed here, but we must attend to only a few of the most sophisticated and
recent examples illustrating the widespread rejection of the post-industrial vision
with its emphasis on information-as-commodity, and the librarian as information
entrepreneur. One example would be the work of William F. Birdsall (1982),
where the author insists that librarianship "must be a politically activist profession" that will battle for free and ready access to information in a democratic society and oppose "fees for service, and the monopolization of information by the
private sector" (p. 226).

Henry Blanke (1989) made the same case in a much commented upon paper
entitled "Librarianship & Political Values." Blanke condemns the post-industrial
vision as a utopia of the right wherein the "introduction of the priorities of the
marketplace will distort the library's traditional function of accumulating and dis-
seminating a wide variety of the world's knowledge as a public good" and have
the effect of creating "an underclass of the information poor" (p. 41). In a more
recent paper Blanke (1990–1991) calls for a critical project that will "enable us to
cut through the rhetoric which rationalizes the introduction of market mechanisms
as the only way for libraries to compete in an entrepreneurial society by making
plain the anti-democratic and inegalitarian implications of such ideas" (p. 13).
This project, Blanke argues, would allow us to "devise strategies to directly intervene in the development of an 'information society' in ways which would further
democratic empowerment and social solidarity rather than private wealth and
privilege" (p. 13).

Finally, in an influential essay, ALA President Patricia Glass Schuman (1990),
called for the rejection of the dangerous "fantasy" that librarians should be "key
players in the information marketplace," for such a course could "lead us to follow the agenda of the marketplace rather than forge our own." She then reminds
librarians that "the production, management, and sale of information is something
quite different from the provision of access" (p. 37). Once again, we find a forceful statement of the neutral, non-prescriptive, library as arsenal of democracy, and

a clear repudiation of the information paradigm (Sosa & Harris, 1991). Most recently, the ALA has endorsed its "ALA Goal 2000," which is designed to better position the Association for the coming fight over free and equitable access to information (Gaughan, 1995). The ALA has invested heavily in its Washington Office in an attempt to influence national information policy, and has actively sought coalitions with other "public interest" groups (St. Lifer & Rogers, 1994).

Of course, this deployment of what appears to be the majority sentiment in the library profession should not be allowed to blind us to the fact that the information paradigm has many powerful supporters in its camp. But it can be argued that the positions of the advocates of the information paradigm are much less consistent than those of their opponents. By that we mean that they tend to fall along a line of support of the information paradigm and reflect both optimism and fear.

The most forceful and optimistic vision is that presented by Lancaster himself. Convinced that Bell's vision of the post-industrial society explained the library future, Lancaster assumed that information-as-commodity was *the product* of the future, and it followed for him that librarians would be literally driven into positions of prominence in the paperless society. Those who resisted this "natural evolution" in the profession would simply become extinct if they continue to cling to nostalgic, obsolete habits of thought and action that prohibit them from changing with the times.

Another large body of support for the information paradigm is based more on fear than optimism. These writers, accepting Bell and Lancaster as guides to the future, nevertheless fear that the transition from paperful to paperless libraries might not be so effortless, and they vigorously insist that librarians are doomed unless they move desperately to "position" themselves advantageously in the post-industrial era. Daniel Carter (1981) saw this clearly when he insisted that libraries and librarians are doomed to a marginal role in the post-industrial society unless they rewrite their official statement. "It is apparent," Carter insists (p. 1386),

> that should no positive redirection, some rewrite of our charter, or redefinition of our objectives take place in the near term, we will be downgraded as a utility in the community by one or more of the emerging alternatives. We can no longer stand on traditional policies, practices, and services. We must change!

Again and again librarians are told that they "must take responsibility for positioning themselves" in the emerging post-industrial society, and a failure to do so will constitute a form of institutional suicide, as the library is "bypassed" in the rush toward an information society (Dowlin, 1980; Woodsworth et al., 1989). "Librarians have long been undervalued," Pat Molholt (1986) notes, but the information paradigm offers "librarians an exciting area in which to carry their profession to a higher level of achievement and recognition" (p. 47). But this evolution is not effortless, Molholt (1988) points out, and those librarians who cannot make the transition to a new role as "knowledge engineer" will be "designed out" (p. 40). "As information professionals," Tom Surprenant (1982a) suggests, "we must be in the forefront of the electronic technology." He argues that "unless we take the initiative, less library-compatible forms of information transfer . . . may emerge," and this "may threaten the existence of the profession itself" (p. 153).

The concerns of these supporters of the information paradigm is clearly self-interested, and should be viewed in the broader context of the librarian's professional project. Thus, we find Pauline Wilson (1978) chiding the ALA for undermining this professional project by resisting the commodification of information. This myopic "intellectual conservatism" only inhibits the development of a "enlarged role in society for their profession" (pp. 128, 124). Linda Main (1990) states the case even more aggressively when she insists that the time for concern with "theoretical and philosophical issues" is past. "What we must be concerned with," Main insists, "is what enables us to survive in a competitive world, namely information technology" (p. 228).

CONCLUSION: LIBRARY AND INFORMATION SERVICES IN THE POST-INDUSTRIAL ERA

Numerous students of the literature on library and information services in the post-industrial era have noticed the disruptive character of the debate. John Berry (1979) precisely identified the problem when he noted that "it is not uncommon for all the disputants to label their views as those most likely to support human freedom" (p. 1732). Perhaps no one has addressed this issue so clearly and productively as the sociologist Irving Horowitz (1991, p. 9) when he observed

> In this nether world, the only admissible allies of democracy are librarians who unabashedly argue the case for free access to information. Behind such pleasantries is the denial that knowledge is a hard-earned value with costs attached to its promulgation no less than its disbursement.

Wishing a pox on both of their houses, Horowitz nonetheless suggests that "it is important to establish ground rules to overcome this current dicotomization between those who insist that every piece of data be paid for and those who argue the free use and disbursement of hard-earned information" (p. 9). Refusing to see the matter as an either/or situation, Horowitz counsels a serious debate about the ways in which we might constructively confront the realities of information production and delivery in the post-industrial era "without sacrificing democratic principles of dissemination or free market principles of supply and demand" (p. 12).

Couched in these terms, the debate takes a more constructive turn, and focuses on John Buschman's (1990) question: "Can we maintain" our commitment to democratic values "through the development of information technology?" Buschman points out that the new technologies are not neutral, but rather have the power to "set limits of what is valuable, informative, socially worthwhile, and logical." "Librarians," he notes, "need to raise and debate these questions in order to recognize alternatives and the kinds of choices involved" (p. 1030).

The foundations of the debate will probably begin with Susan Artandi's (1979) observation that we now live in "an information-rich world in which information is bought, sold, traded, exchanged, and consumed in economic terms." She further notes that information is seen both as "a product and a service" and a life-enhancing tool for human and societal goals (p. 15). In this context librarians cannot simply stand by and await the post-industrial utopia, but rather must recognize that politics *and* economics now play a dominant role in the design and implementation of information services in America. It is no longer constructive to continue the debate in terms of "simple acceptance or rejection" of the commodification of information, for librarians are in no position to make such a decision "unilaterally" (Schiller & Schiller, 1988). The way out may be a recognition of the necessity of accepting the "informatization of society" while at the same time critically thinking through the ways in which libraries can address societal management of information resources in order "to insure that they are maintained and made increasingly available to society at large" (Adams, 1988, p. 36).

What is now quite apparent is that the library profession shares a deep ambivalence toward the post-industrial era. Our ambivalence stems in part from our intuitive sense that there is a "darkside" or "demonic" element in the rush into an information society (Jensen, 1990). Librarians are justified in their concerns about the political assumptions embedded deep within Bell's prophetic vision, but they go too far when they attempt to make the computer into a scapegoat for a much deeper ambivalence about their mission in contemporary society.

It is also clear that a profession is less viable in an environment where traditional loyalties are widely regarded as anachronistic or irrelevant, and that the librarians' professional project will remain stalled without a much higher degree of conscious agreement and commitment to a shared professional ethos. The preceding pages have attempted to demonstrate that the current understandings of the role of the library in society have limited usefulness, and we have attempted to lay the groundwork for a fruitful "second generation" discussion of the essential assumptions that underlay our fundamental beliefs about the mission of the librarian, and the role of libraries, in a capitalist *and* democratic nation. We are asking you, the reader, to engage in the frustrating and risky task of considering not only what libraries do, but why libraries matter.

3

State, Capital, and National Information Policy

In this present crisis, government is not the solution to our problem. Government is the problem.

Ronald Reagan, January 20, 1981

The American people have often complained of the intrusiveness of federal programs, of inadequate performance, and of excessive expenditures. In light of these public concerns, government should consider turning to the creative talents and ingenuity of the private sector to provide, wherever possible and appropriate, better answers to present and future challenges.

Report of the President's Commission on Privatization, 1988

The broadening of information corridors into freeways does not imply that everyone will be able to participate... It will only be so if it is designed to be so. . . . Our community information infrastructure must be less like cable television and more like the public library.

Thomas Hine, 1991

THINKING ABOUT THE ROLE OF THE STATE IN NATIONAL INFORMATION POLICY

Anyone seeking to understand the nature of state intervention in library affairs must do so within what might be appropriately defined as the political economy of national information policy. Political economy, a concept which enjoyed widespread vogue in the 18th and 19th centuries, has only recently been revived as a useful construct for understanding aspects of state intervention in national information policy. It generally connotes the detailed study of the relationship among the state, the economic, and the political order, and suggests a dynamic interdependence among the state, the economy, and the society at large. If we are to make any sense of the role of the state in the formulation of national information policy, and the implications of those policy decisions for library and information services, we must abandon the ingenuous idea that somehow libraries operate in a vacuum, free from the influence of political, economic, and social considerations (Harris & Carrigan, 1990).

THEORIES OF THE STATE

In recent years we have witnessed a renewed interest in theories of the state's role in the affairs of society (Alford & Friedland, 1985; Block, 1987; Carnoy, 1984; Duncan, 1989; Evans, Rueschemeyer, & Skocpol, 1985). For our purposes we might argue that essentially three theories of the state have emerged from this renewed interest and controversy relative to the role of the state in democratic/ capitalist societies: the pluralist view, the instrumentalist view, and the structuralist view. While we cannot concern ourselves with a lengthy discussion of the theoretical issues, it is vital to examine these interpretive frameworks briefly if we are to arm ourselves for the critical exploration of the state's role in formulating contemporary information policy.

The first of these visions is labeled the pluralist theory of the state's role in policy making. It was for many decades the "official ideology" of American political scientists, and one might argue, of Americans in general. As Alford and Friedland (1985) point out, the "pluralist perspective assumes that decision-making processes within the state take place primarily under circumstances of individual political equality and freedom," and it further "assumes that democratic political culture pervades society, and is available to every individual" (p. 36). In pluralist theory the state is seen as a neutral arena for the negotiation of interests. This notion of the state as a neutral agent in the life of a democratic/capitalist nation has always been contested, but has come under increasing attack in the last decade.

The essential critique revolves around the pluralist "claim (very often its implicit assumption) that the major organized 'interests' in these societies . . .

compete on more or less equal terms" in attempting to influence state policy (Miliband, 1969, p. 146). Critics of the pluralist perspective point to the evidence of a distinct asymmetry in the power of different classes to influence state policy. They insist that the pluralist perspective masks this asymmetrical power and has a tendency to distort our understanding of the ways in which the state tends to recognize power in the adjudication of interest group conflicts. In short, they insist that the pluralist perspective tends to privilege equality and liberty in the policy making equation while at the same time rendering the question of asymmetrical power relations "unproblematic."

The increasing uneasiness with the once dominant pluralist vision of the role of the state has given rise to what can be described (for our purposes) as two distinct revisions. The first is the instrumentalist theory, or, as some would suggest, the "class-perspective analysis" of the state (Carnoy, 1984, p. 43). In a strong reaction (or over reaction) to the way in which the pluralist view renders power unproblematic, the instrumentalist theory posits the idea that the state serves the capitalist class because it is directly controlled by that class. That is, it understands the state to be an "instrument" of the capitalist class, and, thus, views state policy as explainable in terms of the interests of the dominant class in the society. Unfortunately, the instrumentalist attempt to compensate for the lack of attention to asymmetrical power in the pluralist theory by privileging the question of power has had a tendency to render the matter of liberty and equality unproblematic.

A third theory, one that has been widely endorsed by social theorists, has arisen in the face of the obvious weaknesses of pluralism and instrumentalism as explanations for state action. This theory, labeled structuralism by its critics and adherents, attempts to transcend these weaknesses by incorporating the character of *liberty* and *power* in the analysis. Insisting that state decision making is neither a simple reflection of power, nor an essentially equal contest, the structuralists (Evans, Rueschemeyer, & Skocpol, 1985, p. viii) claim that "States are potentially autonomous and, conversely, that socioeconomic relations influence and limit state structures and activities."

The key is to come to understand the "conditions favoring or impeding state autonomy, about the determinants of the effectiveness of state interventions, about the unintended consequences of state activities, and about the impact of state policies and structures on social conflicts" (Evans, Rueschemeyer, & Skocpol, 1985, p. viii).

This more productive, and complex, method of interrogating the role of the state in the construction of national information policy offers students of the question a subtle tool for analysis. Perhaps the most influential and useful of the formulations of this structuralist view is that of James O'Connor (1973), who points out that we can only understand the role of the state in a capitalistic society if we acknowledge the centrality of private property. That is, since private property is both the cornerstone of capitalism, and an essential element in our conception of civil liberty, its protection constitutes the state's most powerful focus.

Within this context O'Connor (1973) argues that the state must try to fulfill two basic, and often contradictory, functions at once. He labels these functions as "accumulation" and "legitimation" (p. 6). Simply put, "this means that the state must try to maintain or create the conditions in which profitable capital accumulation is possible," while at the same time the state must also attempt "to maintain or create the conditions for social harmony" (p. 6). These two aspects of state intervention in national information policy are in constant tension. The first is designed to contribute to the orderly (but unregulated) growth of the economy through microeconomic policies through the provision of subsidies to business and industry. The second is designed to insure social stability by making it possible for groups and individuals who are hurt by the workings of the market to meet their basic human needs. This contradictory and dialectical conception appears to provide a particularly fruitful way of thinking about the role of the state in formulating national information policy.

Perhaps the best way to illustrate the value and complexity of O'Connor's model (and to demonstrate its relevance for the library community) is to examine the earliest incarnation of a national information policy as it emerged in the last decade of the 18th century in the United States. Ithiel de Sola Pool (1983) points to the fact that the three fundamental pillars of a national information policy were in place with the ratification of the Constitution in 1789. While those three essential aspects of a national information policy were clearly in their nascent stages, their very simplicity allows us to view the foundations of a national information policy in its purest form and at the same time illustrate the explanatory power of O'Connor's structuralist theory of the state.

Professor Pool pointed out that the founding fathers explicitly addressed the matter of national information policy in three parts of the constitution. First, they allowed (Article 1, Section 8, par. 7) for government intervention in the establishment of post offices and the construction of postroads. This first component of a national information policy clearly played at once both the role of accumulation and legitimation as outlined by O'Connor. Those dedicated to the success of the republican experiment insisted that the rapid and widespread dissemination of the day's intelligence would bind the nation together in political terms, and aid the people in critically participating in their own self-government (John, 1995; Kielbowicz, 1989).

But while many Americans endorsed this construal of power to the federal government in support of enlightened participatory democracy, others eagerly supported the idea based on their desire to see the government subsidize the rapid dissemination of news and advertising, and the efficient distribution of goods, in support of the struggling capitalist system in the early republic. Today, of course, in much more complex and subtle ways various interest groups argue for public subsidies for everything from low postage rates, to government construction of roads and airports, to government investment in the U. S. information industry, for the same contradictory reasons. Librarians, for instance, insist that the postage rates should be kept low in order to facilitate the "free flow" of information, while corporate America insists that the idea of the free flow of information should be extended to cover advertising and "junk mail."

The second pillar of a national information policy that was in place in the Constitution was found in Article 1, Section 8, par. 8, wherein the framers of the Constitution proposed that the government should have the power "to promote the progress of science and useful arts, by securing for limited times to authors and inventors the exclusive right to their respective writings and discoveries." This, the origins of copyright law under the Constitution, provided for the ownership of intellectual property in the service of progress in science and industry. Those librarians who argue that the idea of the "commodification" of information is a totally new idea, do so without the benefit of a reading of the Constitution. While this "power" granted to the Congress of the United States was designed to contribute to conditions in which profitable capital accumulation is possible, it also played a significant role in encouraging the dissemination of information in the United States, and contributed to the legitimation function of state policy as well. It hardly seems necessary to note that the idea of an "information industry" would be inconceivable without the protection of information-as-commodity guaranteed in the copyright provisions of the Constitution.

Finally, the third essential pillar of national information policy is found in what is actually an amendment to the Constitution proper. The First Amendment reads in part "Congress shall make no law . . . abridging freedom of speech or of the press." This, for librarians, the most significant element of the Constitution, is always interpreted as contributing to the democratic process, and is usually defined in strictly political terms. But as has been pointed out by students of this question, the First Amendment is an essential feature of American capitalism since it assures the free flow of information so essential (now more than ever) to the free flow of goods and services. Indeed, it is hard to imagine a capitalist system without protection against undue government interference with the free flow of information.

Ithiel de Sola Pool (1983) rightly suggests that "the constitutional injunctions . . . were thus in appearance somewhat contradictory" due to this dual function of fostering the development of the capitalist economy while at the same time attending to the creation of a just and harmonious society (p. 18). O'Connor's suggestion that the state must always carry out, at one and the same time, both the accumulation function and the legitimation function is clearly demonstrated in the early attention to communications policy in the national charter. And many of the most heated battles in contemporary America relative to communications policy can best be understood as reflecting these contradictory purposes of state intervention in information policy. Later in this chapter we will examine this issue as it explicitly relates to state intervention in library affairs.

But for now we need to note that it appears that the state's role is to reproduce capitalism, and in the United States this has meant that the state must simultaneously play two contradictory roles, that of accumulation and that of legitimation. However, it is also apparent that the state has had a tendency to emphasize one function over another at various times in our history. Indeed, there appears to be an impressively cyclical nature to the process (Schlesinger, 1986). Historians can now point to highly persuasive evidence supporting the claim that the United States has experienced periodic swings of mood, an oscillation between an emphasis on the accumulation function of state policy and the legitimation function. Consider, for instance, the cycle of mood swings from the Progressive Era, to the conservative reaction under Coolidge and Hoover, to the New Deal with its initiation of large scale state intervention on the legitimation side of the ledger, to the conservative swing to an emphasis on accumulation during the 1950s, to the rise of the Great Society under Presidents Kennedy and Johnson, and to the more intense focus on the accumulation function under Reagan and Bush (King, 1993).

Clearly, the maddening complexity and the apparent contradictory nature of much contemporary information policy can be understood within the structuralist framework for interpreting the role of the state. For, as Samuel Bowles and Herbert Gintis (1986) note, the accumulation function is premised on the "preeminence of economic privilege based on property rights" while the legitimation function privileges the "priority of liberty and democratic accountability based on the exercise of personal rights" (p. 3). An awareness of this consistent tension between the accumulation and legitimation function of state information policy, combined with our awareness of the cyclical variations in emphasis on one or the other of these two functions of state policy at different times in our history, prepares us for an examination of state intervention in national information policy in the last two decades of the 20th century.

PRIVATIZATION, FREE MARKETS, AND THE U.S. INFORMATION INDUSTRY

Armed with our model of the state's role in American society we can now begin to think about the direction of state intervention relative to national information policy in the context of the post-industrial era. "Like the industrial revolution, the information revolution is unavoidable," a 1981 report for the Canadian government noted calmly, "consequently, the objectives of public policy should be not to prevent the revolution from occurring, but rather to turn it to our advantage" (Leiss, 1989, p. 283). With this statement we can see the extent and nature of the influence of Daniel Bell's powerful metaphor. As William Leiss (1989) points out, the persuasive power of Bell's metaphor was enormous, and had the power to control and direct government information policy in nations all over the world. Leiss also notes that the stimulus to move quickly grew in urgency over time, "for if serious delays occur the economic advantages of early entry will have been lost, and our society will drift further and further away from the 'action' as each successive wave of innovation rolls in" (Leiss, 1989, p. 283).

Leiss further argues that in the post-industrial era it is widely believed that "public policy is supposed to serve historical inevitability by facilitating a favorable social response to it." As he points out, "if we can be cajoled into believing that some future state is inevitable, and further to alter our behavior in order to conform to its anticipated requirements, the end result will be a retrospective proof of the prediction's accuracy" (pp. 283–284). Leiss concludes that one of the functional objectives of post-industrial theory was to persuade leaders and followers alike to stick to the script, and he provides us with a useful map of this effort at persuasion (p. 284):

- *Analysis* develops a conceptual model, namely, the concept of the 'information society' whose objective is to influence
- *Policy* initiatives that will create favorable conditions for shaping a
- *Social Response* that over time results in changed social behavior and new
- *Behavior Patterns* that resemble those originally predicted as desirable in the
- *Analysis*, thus confirming the model's predictions about what was "inevitable."

In this way Leiss highlights the influence of the state initiatives in national information policy as a powerful force behind the emergence of the "information society" in recent American history. Vincent Mosco (1982) has also detailed the close relationship between the U. S. government and the information industry from the earliest emergence of the computer industry. What is particularly striking, however, is the extent of government intervention since 1980, and the implications this intervention has for national information policy.

THE NEW POLITICS OF INFORMATION

In June of 1979, Walter Wriston, then the Chairman of Citicorp, delivered a speech entitled "Information, Electronics and Gold," in which he described the way in which information technology was revolutionizing our world. "Whether we like it or not," Wriston argued, "mankind now has a completely integrated, international financial and informational marketplace capable of moving money and ideas to any place on this planet within minutes" (quoted in Demac, 1990, p. 207). Chairman Wriston's linkage of money and ideas represents one of the most striking aspects of the new politics of information. For it was increasingly clear, as Vincent Mosco (1982) points out, that the "information sector is replacing manufacturing and agriculture as the major force in the U. S. economy" (p. 46).

Concomitant to this growing conviction that information-as-commodity was the key to future economic growth in the country was the emergence of a new regime in Washington with clearcut inclinations toward the support of the accumulation function in government policy making. The election of Ronald Reagan as the 40th President of the United States in 1980 heralded a dramatic shift in U.S. information policy. In many ways he represented one of the most ideologically committed Presidents to ever occupy the White House. Dedicated to a precise conservative ideology that insisted the government's role in the life of the nation should be strictly limited to the accumulation function, he immediately began to impose his will on national policy. President Reagan and his advisors were committed to a simple vision of laissez-faire economics, and insisted that the government must relinquish its stranglehold on the American economy and let the free market do its magic. President Reagan and his advisors were also persuaded by Daniel Bell's vision of the post-industrial society which would be driven by the emergence of information as *the* commodity capable of fueling a dramatic economic renaissance in America. "America came to be seen," Christopher Lasch (1991) points out, "not as a nation of citizens but of consumers" (p. 68). Deemphasizing the role of the government in the legitimation process, Reagan and his followers focused their policy initiatives on the needs and interests of the high technology component of the U.S. economy.

Before we examine the ways in which this convergence of the information society with the ideological inclinations of the regime currently in power in Washington impacted national information policy we must pause for a brief historical examination of three recent examples of government intervention in national library affairs. The first, the massive state support for library services initiated under the Kennedy and Johnson administrations, and the second, and equally dramatic, attempt on the part of the Reagan and Bush administrations to redirect the state's role relative to libraries while at the same time explicitly attempting to redefine the very purpose of libraries in the context of national information policy, and finally, the emergence of what we call the "First Post-Industrial Democrats"—Bill Clinton and Al Gore.

LEGITIMATION AND ACCUMULATION IN STATE INFORMATION POLICY

In 1944, Fremont Rider, the Librarian at the Wesleyan University Library, declared the startling fact that his study of academic libraries in the United States revealed that they were actually doubling in size every 16 years. Rider concluded that if these growth rates were projected into the future the results were "astronomical," and clearly could not be supported by the nation's library system. His solution, a paperless library based on the new technology of the microcard, seemed rational enough but fell on deaf ears among the members of the library and book community. How, it might be asked, could the library community blink the facts, how could they comfortably assume that they could continue to raise the resources necessary to acquire the materials and build the buildings necessary to house these dramatically increased holdings? The answer was—obvious from our present vantage point—that librarians fully expected massive intervention from outside sources, hopefully the federal government, to supply the necessary funds. And, their expectation was indeed met.

As early as the late 1940s forces were set in motion that were designed to encourage federal intervention in the support of libraries. At this time, many observers began to sense the intense symbiotic relationship that had developed between American libraries and the high culture publishing industry in America. It was becoming increasingly clear that libraries of all kinds had become essential markets for the consumption of serious literature, scholarly publications in book and periodical form, and "quality" children's books. Indeed, it was already obvious that libraries represented literally the only market for much of this material, and in time publishers of this material came to see the American library system as an essential subsidy to scholarly and high culture publishing and concomitantly to the research and literary progress of the country (M. H. Harris, 1986a; Harris & Carrigan, 1990). The widespread clamor for cooperation, or the introduction of non-book formats, threatened the destruction of the close relationship between libraries and the high culture industry, while at the same time promising a dramatic restructuring of both institutions. In the face of this threat powerful forces were marshalled to find the resources necessary to alleviate the space and financial problems facing the nation's libraries.

The agenda for the forces of the book was quite clear. First, convince the national government to supply resources for the construction of hundreds of libraries across the land (ultimately it was thousands) that would, for a time, eliminate the space problem that Rider predicted, and block all discussion of cutting back on library acquisitions or eliminating the book altogether. Second, gain support for federal funding for the acquisition of library materials. Third, encourage support for the training of professional librarians and provide funds for the employment of these same librarians.

Library users found this agenda quite to their liking. After all, users saw libraries as essentially repositories for the printed word. Any proposal that would enhance access to library materials would be expected to gain their support. Librarians, educated in the humanities and dedicated to the high culture mission of the library in American society, were also eager to support the program. Besides, it would clearly attack the central problems facing libraries at the time: crowding, squeezed acquisitions budgets, and a shortage of staff. Of course, it would allow the profession to deal with these problems without confronting the jarring implications of Rider's suggested paperless library. In short, despite Rider's dire predictions, it could be business as usual.

All that remained was to convince the government (Congress and the president) of the need for massive federal intervention in library affairs. This task was successfully completed with apparent ease. First came the passage of the Library

Services Act in 1956, a bill designed to extend library service to rural Americans through state and public libraries. This act was amended in 1965 as the Library Services and Construction Act. The two acts taken together resulted in federal expenditure of some $425 million for books and staff salaries, and some $168 million for library construction by 1974. Then came Title II of the Elementary and Secondary Education Act, which provided some $750 million for the acquisition of library materials by 1974. This bill was quickly followed by Title II-A of the Higher Education Act, which provided some $150 million in federal monies for academic library acquisitions through 1975. Another $40 million was expended for the training of professional librarians, principally under the provisions of the National Defense Education Act and the Higher Education Act. While estimates vary as to the exact extent of federal investment in libraries, a conservative figure would be somewhere around $2 billion from 1956 to 1980. This enormous windfall effectively alleviated the space, acquisitions, and staffing problems of libraries (at least for the time being) and constituted the most significant growth in library support ever experienced in this country.

How could such an enormous federal intervention in library affairs have come about? We have already alluded to the powerful coalition of forces in the book community that came together to lobby for the passage of legislation to support the status quo in libraries. But the key to the success of these programs appears to lie in the general endorsement for the library projects by Presidents Kennedy and Johnson.

It is now clear that the proposals for national support of library programs were grounded in a liberal ideology that insisted that the success of the American experiment depends on the enlightened participation of the people in the political process, and argues that widespread and enlightened participation requires easy and equitable access to information defined as a public good (Dervin, 1994; Molz, 1976). Quite simply, both Kennedy and Johnson agreed that the state had a moral responsibility to facilitate the development of an educated and civically virtuous citizenry, and they were persuaded that libraries could contribute in a significant way to this vital national project. That they were capable of providing such massive support was in part due to the general health of the economy (a shortlived condition) and the aggressive pressure brought to bear on the two Presidents and Congress by the high culture lobby.

The success of the high culture lobby brought with it substantial liabilities for the library profession. The massive support for the acquisition of books and periodicals, the construction of buildings, and the training of book people to be librarians firmly embedded the American library system in the high culture industry, and made its commitment to library service as a "public good" all the more intense. It is increasingly clear the library profession's power to direct its own destiny had been effectively circumscribed by this development. From the mid-1960s, the library's structural and functional characteristics were determined by its definition as an institution contrived to consume, preserve, transmit, and reproduce high culture in printed form as a public good (Harris, 1986a). Dan Lacy (1978, p. 31) clearly understood this development when he noticed that such massive government intervention had dramatically impacted not just libraries but the process of knowledge production itself:

> It has done so not by utilizing its sovereign power to override the marketplace, but rather by entering that marketplace itself as the most important provider and the most important buyer of information disseminated through print . . . . For decades this steady flow of publicly funded demand has supported the publication of textbooks, of children's books, of many kinds of reference and other non-fiction books primarily of library interest, and, at the college and university level, of university press publications and other advanced scholarly and scientific books and journals. The relative abundance of this support in the United States has shaped the publishing industry quite differently from that of a country like Italy or Spain or France, where the industry primarily serves private demand.

This choice of allegiances was to prove a serious problem at the dawn of the "post-industrial era" and the election of a series of Presidents whose ideologies did not cover federal support for cultural intervention in the life of the nation.

Changed attitudes towards government intervention in national information policy began to emerge during the presidency of Richard Nixon, but the election of Ronald Reagan as the President of the United States heralded a dramatic shift in federal policy towards libraries. He was adamant in his insistence that the federal government had no right to interfere in local affairs, and that it was the right and responsibility of local governments to direct their own destinies across the whole range of social and cultural concerns.

Further, he reflected an intense commitment to an ideology of laissez-faire economics, and insisted that the government must relinquish its strangle hold on the American economy. President Reagan and his advisors were also quite taken, as was the society at large, with Daniel Bell's vision of the "Post-Industrial Society," which would be driven by the emergence of information as a commodity capable of fueling a dramatic economic recovery in America. In the context of his firm ideological commitments and his conviction that Bell was on to something the President proposed a number of policy initiatives that were to have widespread ramifications for the society at large, and more specifically for the nation's libraries.

Despite congressional opposition this ideological vision took tangible shape in the form of significant tax cuts directed at the upper strata of American society; cuts in social programs; deliberate attempts to deregulate American industry; and the provision of a package of subsidies to American industry. For the American library system this ideological blitzkrieg had ominous overtones.

The President and his advisors soon made it clear that they had no intention to support local library services with federal monies. Whatever public sector support libraries might receive would now be expected to be allocated from local resources. President Reagan not only proved indifferent to appeals for federal support for libraries, but actually took a hostile stand. Further, he insisted that information as a commodity was the key to future economic development in the country, and quickly made it clear that he intended to nurture the private sector information industry, while casting an indifferent eye on the political and cultural aspirations of the public sector library and information services in the United States (Harris & Carrigan, 1990).

PRESIDENT CLINTON AS THE FIRST POST-INDUSTRIAL DEMOCRAT

Then, in 1992, the election of Democratic presidential candidate Bill Clinton encouraged all who hoped for a return to a firm national commitment to the idea that information should be viewed as a public good. For historically it was the Democrats who had been most willing to endorse the liberal notion of information as a public good that had made the U. S. government at once the largest buyer of information and the largest producer of information in the world. However, those hoping for a return of widespread government intervention in the provision of information to the people were quickly disappointed, for Bill Clinton and especially his vice president, Al Gore, were persuaded that Daniel Bell's blueprint for the future of America was correct and quickly moved to support the private sector development of the information marketplace.

While the president and vice president made passionate speeches in support of the idea of free access to information, they placed most of the power over the emerging information highway in the hands of Secretary of Commerce Ron Brown whose sympathies were decidedly pro business. The priorities of the Administration were nicely articulated in Vice President Gore's plan for the National Information Infrastructure (NII) in which he admitted that the concern for public access to information ranked second to the government's desire to "promote private sector investment in the NII." The dominance of the Commerce Department in formulating national communications policy signaled the continued control of the policy making process by the U. S. information industry. Especially troubling to librarians was the virtual lack of reference to libraries in the policy documents spelling out the future of the NII (Henry, 1994).

The administration moved with such urgency in 1993 that they created a "firestorm" of awareness and controversy relative to the nature of the emerging information economy in the United States (Hernon, McClure, & Relyea, 1996; Maule, 1994; Sprehe, 1994). However, it soon became clear that the majority of the administrative initiatives in the area of national communication policy would be tilted towards the private sector of the economy and that information as a public good would be replaced with the notion of information as a commodity to be sold on markets—in short, the emphasis seemed to be on the privatization of the production and dissemination of information in the United States. The effects on the public library system are still unclear, but the long-term implications are ominous. What we appear to be witnessing is the emergence of what we want to call the *First Post-Industrial Democrats*; that is, Democrats who have generally repudiated the notion of information as a public good and embraced the idea that information is now the key commodity in the economy and have therefore concluded that its production and dissemination should be privatized. The role of government becomes primarily one of supporting the emerging U. S. information industry in ways that will insure U.S. domination of the world information marketplace.

Using Pool's (1983) typology of the key elements of a national communications policy, we can outline a tentative assessment of the future of information in the United States and the implications of these trends for the American public information system. Let us begin with the first of Pool's categories: the government's right to manage the national information infrastructure. It has been in this area, of course that the Clinton administration has moved most dramatically and visibly to stimulate the growth of the U. S. information industry. In their Agenda for National Information Infrastructure Development (1993) the Clinton administration announced its desire to foster the growth of the U. S. information economy via tax incentives and relaxed regulatory policies; the auctioning off of radio spectrum to the private sector for wireless communication systems; and the provision of direct subsidies to the private sector for the development and deployment of new information technology.

The government also made it clear that it would move aggressively to open foreign markets for U. S. information goods and services and systematically punish those countries that might attempt to stifle the emerging U. S. information industry. Much of this activity was carried out under the general umbrella of the National Information Infrastructure (NII) Act of 1993 which contributed significantly to initiatives designed to integrate the "hardware, software and skills necessary to the creation of a national digital information system that will efficiently and cost-effectively allow the integration of the national communications system."

The government's efforts to deregulate the marketplace proceeded with remarkable speed and resulted in a massive revision of national communications policy with the passage of the Telecommunications Act of 1996, which was labeled a bill designed to

> provide for a pro-competitive, de-regulatory national policy framework designed to accelerate rapidly private sector deployment of advanced telecommunications and information technologies and services to all Americans by opening all telecommunications markets to competition and for other purposes.

This legislation was designed to break down boundaries between markets like cable television and local telephone service that had traditionally been monopolies in individual markets. The broader goal, was in the Vice-President's words, aimed at the removal "over time . . . of judicial and legislative restrictions on all types of telecommunications companies" (Quoted in Pavlik, 1996, p. 255). The government's desire to facilitate the private sector's investment in the NII has also lead to a systematic relaxation of anti-trust concerns. The upshot has been a dramatic consolidation of the various components of the industry as strategists struggle to create mega-companies that will be competitive in the new de-regulated marketplace.

Observers have been startled at the speed and magnitude of these mergers as one massive deal after another moves through the system. One recent example is the $7.5 billion combination of Time Warner and Turner Broadcasting despite the fears of media watchers who insisted that such a massive merger would dramatically reduce the variety of programming available to American cable television viewers.

The movement to consolidate in order to be competitive in the new information marketplace continues in the United States, but already some 1,500 deals worth nearly $150 billion have been consummated, deals that represent an enormous consolidation of the industry. Such a systematic and widespread conglomeration of the information industry raises many fears among those who see a steadily diminishing pool of voices in the industry. This massive combination of resources coupled with the deregulation of the communications industry leads many civil libertarians to conclude that we may be witnessing the abandonment of the notion of the common carrier—the obligation to maintain a public conduit for a free flow of information that is open to everyone. They also fear the emerging ability of large conglomerates to control both the conduit and the content might stifle competition, content diversity, and even, they argue, free speech.

The Clinton administration has also moved aggressively to "reinvent government" in a leaner and more efficient form. Several areas of reform that have had a significant impact on national communications policy have been the continued support for the paperwork reduction plan implemented by earlier administrations and carried out primarily by the Office of Management and Budget (OMB). The OMB initiatives have recommended a reduction in the amount of government involvement in information gathering and dissemination, and we appear to be moving towards a moment when Dan Lacy's conclusion that the federal government is the largest producer and consumer of information in the world is no longer true. In one of the most dramatic moves to date, Congress voted in 1995 to cut federal support for the Depository Library Program in the United States, and in a reflection of its conviction that digital communication systems represent the future, they mandated a massive shift from print dissemination to electronic dissemination beginning in 1996. Congress later decided to restore much of this funding, and concluded that the Federal Depository Library Program can have until 2002 to make the transition to a totally digital dissemination system. However, some components have moved with more speed. The National Library of

Agriculture has already announced that all of its publications will be in digital formats in the future.

Critics, of course, insist that changes in the collection and delivery of information as a public good will undermine the process of informed political deliberation so fundamental to the success of the democratic society—in short they see these attempts at efficiency and cost-effectiveness as veiled attempts to undermine democracy.

While all of these moves by the Clinton administration have proven valuable stimulants to the development of the U. S. information industry, they have lead to a steady erosion of government support for the public delivery of information services in the United States. The Clinton administration, surprisingly to some, significantly cut library support, just as the Reagan/Bush administrations had done before them. As Betty Turock (1994, p. 126) has indicated, "Even with the long-awaited Clinton administration in power, the fate of libraries has not improved." Historically, Congress has frequently refused to accept the President's suggestions for zero support for libraries and the grant programs remain quite popular (Fuller, 1994). However, the ever-weaker position of the idea of information as public good is seen in a series of recent developments such as the passage of a draconian increase in postal rates (1995) for library materials which will clearly force cuts in interlibrary loan services in public libraries, and the degree to which librarians are being ignored for appointment to important policy-making bodies.

Another observer (Branscomb, 1995, p. 18) recently put it this way:

> If you read between the lines of the Clinton Administration's efforts to define a national information infrastructure (NII), although there is an admonition to the private sector to link schools, libraries and hospitals to the information superhighway . . . the primary purpose of the NII is to assure the United States of a global competitive advantage.

Another perspective from which we might attempt to assess the Clinton administration's tendencies in information policy would be to look at the question from the point of view of Professor Pool's second pillar of national communication policy: that is, the protection of information as a commodity. A number of the most noteworthy students of the information economy have repeatedly made the point that the notion of information as commodity is impossible without a strong and effective copyright law, and thus a strong copyright law is a key element in any effort to grow the U. S. information economy.

Historians of copyright notice that Americans waited almost 70 years after accepting the 1909 Copyright Act before passing a major revision in 1976. However, the emergence of information technology and digital communications systems in the 1980s was already provoking many to call for another and much more radical revision of the law to meet the needs of the information industry in the post-industrial era (Patterson & Lindberg, 1991). While the Reagan and Bush administrations spent some time considering a revision of the Copyright Law it was the Clinton administration that moved most aggressively to guarantee property rights in information. Insisting that the information industry and its needs should and would dictate national information policy, Secretary Brown, organized a Working Group on Intellectual Property to consider revisions to the 1976 law. And, in the fall of 1995, the Task Force, chaired by Commissioner of Patents and Trademarks Bruce Lehman, issued a 240-page White Paper designed to provide enhanced protection for digital information commodities as we enter the 21st century.

Once again, the Clinton administration's tilt towards the needs of the information industry became apparent, and furthermore, remarks made by Secretary Brown suggested the reasons for the Administration's policy. When the White Paper was released it was Brown who noted that it was the Administration's intent to accelerate the Internet's metamorphosis from an "intriguing communications tool" into a "cybermarketplace" where "customers" will buy information goods and services from producers, and, ultimately, Brown said, the goal is to develop the Internet into a "system for international commerce." And of course, the administration was encouraged in its quest by figures like Bill Gates (1995, p. 6), the president of Microsoft, who insists that "digital information of all kinds . . . will be the new medium of exchange in this market," and that "the global information market will be huge."

The administration makes it very clear that it feels, in agreement with Daniel Bell's predictions, that information will become the commodity of the 21st century, that information technology is the "critical technology" of the future and that the U. S. information industry will be the engine that will power the U. S. economy to a position of world leadership (L. Branscomb, 1993). In the context of that feeling it is little wonder that it has moved so aggressively to protect intellectual property rights.

This also explains the amazing risks the administration was willing to take when it threatened to impose sanctions on China in retaliation for the Chinese penchant for pirating billions of dollars of American information products. That is, observers were startled to see the U.S. risking a trade war with China over "intellectual property rights," but those familiar with the information policy trajectory of the first post-industrial democrats, were not a bit surprised. After all, if information as commodity is going to be the key commodity of the "cybermarketplace" it follows that the U. S. government must protect this vital commodity in the world marketplace. And careful students of the world economy know how copyright issues are now becoming key elements in setting the foreign policy priorities of the developed countries in the West. "The 'sanctity of intellectual property'," notes James Boyle (1996, p. 3), "has come to play an iconic role in the foreign policy of the developed world similar to the role played by 'freedom of the seas' . . . in an earlier age." Many have also noticed that the United States is attempting to dictate the revision of the Berne Convention covering international copyright protection.

The administration's spirited defense of intellectual property rights as we enter the 21st Century threatens to "turn the notion of fair use on its head" and has provoked many librarians and advocates of user rights to stridently oppose the changes. Long-time proponents of the rights of the public, librarians in the U. S. are continuing to vocalize their opposition to any legislation that would reduce the terms of fair use (Association of Research Libraries, 1995; Crews, 1993). Fearing that the interests of the publishers will be given greater attention, there is strong resistance to the notion of licensing requirements, which many librarians note, could easily result in the library patron being forced to pay for reading anything electronic. Coupled with the considerable cost for equipment, the proposed reforms could effectively increase the ever-widening gap between the information rich and information poor. Librarians are also quick to point out how this situation will only be exacerbated by the continuing decrease in library funding. James Boyle (1996) put it nicely when he noted that if the proposed bill were to become law "the information superhighway will become an information toll road" (p. 135).

Directly related to the rise of information as commodity in the new information marketplace are issues related to rights of privacy in the post-industrial era. Two powerful drivers—the new information technology and the increasing value of information as a commodity—have stimulated a massive surge of information gathering that threatens the privacy of every American. This market driven surveillance of our private consumption habits has not yet reached Orwellian proportions, but it is clear that the new information technology has the potential to force a reconceptualization of the notion of privacy (Boyle, 1996, p. 4).

On balance the last several administrations in Washington have appeared to view privacy laws as anti-business, and this sentiment has been intensified as information is elevated to the position of the key commodity in the marketplace. Corporate interests then develop a urgent need to gather and add value to information, much of that information, of course, relating to the lives of individuals. We now find ourselves entering an era when corporate America, aided by new information technology and supported by the government, "compiles, modifies, redesigns, and commodifies information gleaned in part from [their] genes, consumption patterns, and culture" (Boyle, 1996, p. 177).

Thus, corporate interests are demanding the right to acquire and manage information without government interference, and legislation is currently being considered that seems to tilt towards the interests of the private sector. Once again the interests of the private sector and the public interest seem to be in conflict, and it can be concluded that the Clinton administration's stance in this area is decidedly "post-industrial," that is, all decisions are now being made in the context of the belief that the information industry represents the future of the U. S. economy and therefore must be nurtured at all costs. This ideology explains the administration's willingness to embrace the notion that huge amounts of data on individuals must be gathered, organized, and shared in order to fuel the new information economy effectively. Of course, the die is not completely cast, and a wide range of privacy advocates are now fully mobilized and in the field in an attempt to reverse current trends and establish effective curbs on corporate and government invasions of privacy (Branscomb, 1994; Gandy, 1993; Regan, 1995; Smith, 1994). Librarians, always forceful advocates of patron privacy, stand, of course, with the civil libertarians. However, at this moment the privatization and commercialization of information are proving so dynamic a movement that our forward progress towards what Oscar Gandy (1993) has labeled the "Panoptic Sort" would appear inevitable.

Still following Pool we need to examine the current condition of information services in America from one further perspective, and that was the notion of intellectual freedom, or more precisely, the free flow of information. In this area we can be quite concise. This, for librarians, the most significant element of the Constitution, is always interpreted as contributing to the democratic process, and is usually defined in strictly political terms. But as has been pointed out by students of this question, the first amendment is an essential feature of American capitalism since it assures the free flow of information so essential (now more than ever) to a free market system. Indeed, it is hard to imagine a capitalist system without protection against undue government interference with the free flow of information. This is particularly true when "information" has become the central commodity in the global economy.

On balance the Clinton administration seems to be fully aware of the need to secure a free marketplace of information commodities. However, the President is also faced with considerable social and political pressures that are in many ways too complex to be discussed here. Let it be said, however, that while insisting that the administration is in favor of the free flow of ideas, President Clinton has also put pressure on the movie industry in an attempt to eliminate violence from films; signed a Communications Act that contained a very restrictive anti-obscenity provision; and generally has been very critical of pornography (Clinton, 1996). It may be impossible to see where the administration is going in this area, but there is no question where corporate America stands. Powerful figures such as Microsoft's Bill Gates are highly visible in insisting that digital commodities should be allowed to find customers without government interference. The question, always far from clear, boils down once again to free speech expert Zechariah Chafee's conclusion when pressed for a final assessment of U. S. policy on intellectual freedom: "We will allow what we will allow," he said.

Perhaps the most significant effect of the rise of post-industrialism, and far and away its most disturbing feature for those who advocate on behalf of the 10,000 public libraries in America, is the implication that the system should be privatized. This proposal implies that the government is not capable of effectively managing the nation's communication system, and that the private sector is. All arguments to the contrary seem to be viewed as unconvincing and the government continues to diminish government support quietly for information in the public sector, including information delivered through libraries.

Critics of the movement to privatize information delivery in the U. S. are quick to point out that such a movement will inevitably broaden the gap between the information rich and the information poor in America, and thus further oppress those who are in America's lower classes (Kahin & Keller, 1995; Wresch, 1996). That is, if knowledge is power, then surely the rich will be further empowered by reason of their ability to acquire large amounts of information on the private marketplace (Birdsall, 1994; Buschman, 1995; H. Schiller, 1996).

The final conclusion to be drawn is that in the U. S., information has been declared the commodity that will power the economy towards continued dominance of world markets well into the 21st century. Both Democratic and Republican regimes in Washington now seem to agree that the U. S. information industry holds great promise and, thus, have shown a great interest in nurturing the industry. This intense interest in creating a world-wide market for U. S. information industry products and services promises to further undermine the notion of information as a public good that should be provided to all on an equal basis as the foundation of a democratic society. Such an idea, once so central to the American political credo, is no longer widely accepted, and this reality would suggest that the public library system is in danger of loosing its hallowed position as the "Arsenal of Democratic Culture" as the United States emerges as the First Post-Industrial Democracy.

DEMONIZED ADVERSARIES: PRIVATIZATION

The situation takes on even more clarity when one examines the conservative project that came to take on at least symbolic centrality in the arsenal of the critics of the government's role in the provision of information services as a public good. Privatization became a rallying cry for those who attributed most of the nation's problems to "Big Government" (Bruchey, 1990). "Two political legacies of the 1980s color and constrain the economic policies of the 1990s," John Donahue (1989, p. 3) notes

> One is a renewed cultural enthusiasm for private enterprise. The other is an endur-
> ing, deficit-induced imperative to limit government spending. The confluence of
> these two trends had led to great hopes and claims for "privatization," the practice
> of delegating *public* duties to *private* organizations.

Albert O. Hirschman (1991, p. 7) suggests that conservatives deployed three fundamental theses in their attack on Big Government. Hirschman calls them "the *perversity thesis*, or thesis of the perverse effect, the *futility thesis*, and the *jeopardy thesis*":

> According to the *perversity* thesis, any purposive action to improve some feature of the political, social, or economic order only serves to exacerbate the condition one wishes to remedy. The *futility* thesis holds that attempts at social transformation will be unavailing, that they will simply fail to 'make a dent.' Finally, the *jeopardy* thesis argues that the cost of the proposed change or reform is too high as it endangers some previous, precious accomplishment.

All three of these theses are aggressively deployed in the celebrated *Report of the President's Commission on Privatization* (Linowes, 1988, p. vii) when it is noted in the "Preface" that

> The American people have often complained of the intrusiveness of federal programs, of inadequate performance, and of excessive expenditures. In light of these public concerns, government should consider turning to the creative talents and ingenuity in the private sector to provide, wherever possible and appropriate, better answers to present and future challenges.

In its review of government activities the Commission asked a series of questions: "Are there extensive complaints of poor or insufficient service," is there evidence of waste, is the government involved in unfair and counterproductive competition with the private sector "by relying on subsidies" (p. viii)? Noting that its efforts were stimulated by a "renewed interest in the systematic examination of the boundary between public and private delivery of goods and services" provoked by widespread agreement that "the federal government has become too large, too expensive, and too intrusive in our lives" the Commission declares that its mission is to "assess the range of activities that might properly be transferred to the private sector and to investigate methods by which such a shift could be accomplished" (p. 1).

The *Report* then turns to an outline and discussion of the various ways in which this mission might be undertaken: (1) sale or other forms of divesture of government assets, (2) contracting out government services, and (3) the creation of a voucher system "under which the government distributes purchasing power to eligible consumers" (pp. 1–2). The Commission also notes that "user fees" that "place the burden of paying for the public service on those who benefit from it, rather than on taxpayers in general" is also part of the privatization arsenal. Noting that the American privatization effort is part of a worldwide movement, the Commission argues that "we have just begun" the effort to stimulate "a renewed reliance on the talents and ingenuity of private citizens to develop better ways to accomplish what is now government's business" (p. 6). The last chapter of the *Report* (pp. 250–251) is a concise restatement of the purpose and commitment of the forces supporting the deemphasis of the state's legitimation function:

The ultimate consequences of the new forces at work today in American political and economic life, including whether these forces will be longer lasting or shorter lived, will not be seen for some time. What can be said is that the privatization movement is likely to be at the center of the response to these forces. In seeking to reduce the role of government and to rely more heavily on the private sector, the privatization movement is a reflection of the failure of many of the past assumptions on which large government has been based.

While this argument is based on many "assumptions" that would appear to be flawed, the fact remains that the conclusion that "the privatization movement is likely to be at the center" of all future discussions of the role of the state does appear to be correct (Donahue, 1989; Henig, 1994; Starr, 1988; Weisbrod, 1988).

Jeffrey R. Henig (1989–1990, p. 669) argues that library interests would be well advised to remind themselves that the argument is *political* as well as economic:

> The theory underlying privatization is significant because it represents a deliberate effort to redefine both economic and political interests. And it has been successful, at least in the sense that it has reshaped political discourse. Governmental options are conceived and talked about differently today. The differences shift expectations and the burden of proof against those who would argue for an authoritative governmental role.

THE CURRENT PROSPECT: PROGRESS OR DESPAIR

We must now attempt to provide a sober assessment of this changed environment that will contribute to a reasonable plan of action. What is needed is a vision that will transcend the fatalistic pessimism and wistful optimism so prevalent in our thinking on the role of the library in the information society. Perhaps the way to begin is to present a thorough and evenhanded description of the ideological underpinnings of the Reagan and Bush initiatives relative to national information policy. At the outset we need to recall the increasing awareness among Reagan and his advisors that information was becoming a commodity, "not just *any* commodity, either, but a fundamental source of growth for the market system as a whole; information, some say, has become the essential site of capital accumulation within the world economy" (D. Schiller, 1988, p. 27). The implications of this transformation was spelled out by countless business leaders, but IBM Vice-President Lewis Branscomb summed it all up well in the *New York Times* (August 20, 1981) when he noted that the emergence of information as the *central* commodity in the post-industrial era heralded "a deep transformation in which information is purveyed as an economic good, rather than as a social overhead."

Perhaps the best way to highlight the speed and velocity with which the change took place is to notice that in 1975 The National Commission of Library and

Information Science (NCLIS), created in 1970 under the Nixon administration, issued a report reflecting its views on the long-term goals of a national information policy. At that time the NCLIS still showed a strong commitment to the creation of "information justice" via state subsidies to the public sector information delivery system. However, it was already clear in 1975 that the free-market forces were growing more robust as evidenced by the remark that "the information industry will exert increased influence on the nation's information services in the years ahead" (p. 25). Just one year later NCLIS published the report of the Domestic Council Committee on the Right of Privacy (1976), chaired by Nelson Rockefeller, which heralded a dramatic shift in emphasis with the "voice and perspective of the information industry" emerging forcefully. This report moved aggressively to position the NCLIS in the information industry camp and outlined a plan for dismantling the "national structure of public information supply and enable private information interests to become its expropriators" in support of a climate conducive to information industry "growth and investment" (H. Schiller & A. Schiller, 1988, p. 157).

Far and away the most significant landmark in the rapid transit from the legitimation to the accumulation function as the dominant theme in U. S. information policy was the report entitled *Public Sector/Private Sector Interaction in Providing Information Services*, published by NCLIS in 1982, and dealing with the "emerging national debate on the appropriate role of the public and private sectors in the United States." The Task Force responsible for writing the report was charged with the responsibility of considering this question in the light of two fundamental assumptions (p. v):

1. The crucial importance of information resources, products, and services in our economy and society.
2. The conflicting views concerning the proper role of government in providing those information resources, products, and services.

Early in the *Report* it is noted that the Task Force was divided in its commitments, and "basic differences" existed resulting in "conflicts between restricting and not restricting the role of government" (p. viii). In what is perhaps the clearest summary of the principles underlying the post-industrial commitment to information-as-commodity, the Task Force (pp. viii-ix) notes that those in favor of limiting the state's role in information service deploy the following arguments:

1. Our society is founded on the traditional view that individual freedom and initiative, expressed through competitive private enterprise, are the best means of supplying the products and services needed by society.
2. Government entry into the marketplace can have a chilling effect on private sector investment in the generation, collection, and distribution of information.

3.   When the government enters the marketplace, it interferes with the ability of the market mechanism to allocate resources to the optimum production of goods and services.
4.   The private sector, if not threatened by the anti-competitive effects of government in the marketplace, can widen the distribution of information from the government as well as other sources.

Recalling Hirschman's (1991) notion of three principle critiques of state intervention in the life of the nation, we can constructively point to the extent to which the *Report* deploys the perversity, futility, and jeopardy theses. *Perversity*, if government subsidizes information service as a "public good" it will only make things worse; *futility*, if the government intervenes it will not make a "dent" in the problem; or *jeopardy*, if the government subsidizes information service it will undermine a much higher value—individual freedom. In this reading of the role of the state, it is also apparent that the classic laissez-faire doctrine of citizenship is strongly in play, and that Christopher Lasch's (1991) conclusion that in this frame we tend to see America as a nation of "consumers" not "citizens" is strongly supported.

In fairness the Task Force also outlined the principles underlying the argument that the government should aggressively engage in the creation and distribution of information as a "public good." These principles included an emphasis on the extent and nature of "market failure" and the fundamental idea that the state had an obligation to facilitate the development of "informed" citizens "regardless of their individual ability to pay for needed information" (p. ix).

While the Task Force was divided, and clearly encountered much controversy in the pursuit of its objectives, it nevertheless presented a series of recommendations relative to the state's role in the information society that heralded the dramatic shift in state policy from legitimation to accumulation. The executive summary (p. v) makes this tendency perfectly clear when it notes that the *Report* is concerned with the following major issues:

1.   The need for the Federal government to take a position of leadership in facilitating the development and fostering the use of information products and services. As part of that, the open dissemination of information from governmental activities should be regarded as a high priority responsibility, especially through private sector means.
2.   Private sector investment in information resources, products, and services should be encouraged and not discouraged. As part of that, libraries and other information activities in the private sector should be used as the means for distribution of information from the federal government, in preference to using newly created government agencies.
3.   The government should not engage in commercial information activities unless there are compelling reasons for it to do so, and there must be well

defined procedures for determining that such reasons indeed are present. Prices for government products and services should be consistent with the actual costs for making the information available.

4.   If private sector information is included in any package of governmentally distributed information the private sector property rights should be carefully protected.

Nowhere in the *Report* are any proposals made to increase state support for the public sector information delivery system, and scattered throughout the document are more or less explicit suggestions that funding should be cut (Schuman, 1982).

"With the publication of this report," Herbert and Anita Schiller note, "it was clear that the balance had moved decisively toward the commercial information industry and away from the principle of information as a social good." They conclude that the *Report* "may be read as a declaration of the industry's triumph in the information arena" (Schiller & Schiller, 1988, p. 159; Smith, 1985). Miriam Braverman (1982) ominously declared that "a specter is haunting this country—the specter of Adam Smith" (p. 397). Thus, we see in the *Report* the degree to which the combination of the emergence of information as the key commodity in the information era and the laissez-faire ideology of the ascendent regime in Washington fused into a powerful force for change in the nature of national information policy, and constituted a deliberate attempt to redefine the role of the library in the post-industrial era.

LIBRARIES IN THE ERA OF INFORMATION AS COMMODITY

The impact of this altered understanding of the role of the state in national information policy had immediate and far reaching impacts on the profession. Condemning the "simplistic and dangerous approach" endorsed by NCLIS, Patricia Glass Schuman (1982) rehearsed all of the professions longstanding justifications for state support for the public sector provision of information in a democratic society. Admitting that "satisfactorily merging questions of information access and social justice with economic profit and progress is not a simple task" she insisted that the essential premise informing the debate should be that "equal access to information is a natural extension of democratic principles" and should not be compromised (p. 1066). Further, librarians have also had the benefit of careful and critical analyses of the question of information as a public or private good (Detlefson, 1984; McCain, 1988).

Literally hundreds of articles and official American Library Association documents have been published in support of the "article of faith that people should not have to pay for access to public information" (Rochell, 1985, p. 6). Librarians are constantly encouraged to do battle for the free and ready access to information in a democratic society and oppose "fees for service and the monopolization of information by the private sector" (Birdsall, 1982, p. 226). Many have noticed "that the introduction of the priorities of the marketplace will distort the library's traditional function" of delivering information as a "public good," and the profession is exhorted to fight on against all odds in the service of democracy and "information justice" (Blanke, 1989, p. 41). Always the theme is the same, for "surely, we cannot allow the creation, dissemination, and preservation of knowledge to become a decision of the marketplace" (Rochell, 1987, p. 48).

In 1985, The Council of Library Resources (quoted in Shiller & Shiller, 1988, p. 162) put it even more forcefully:

Ways must be found to assure continuing attention for those aspects of culture and learning that are important but, in a commercial sense, not necessarily in fashion . . . Uncritical adherence to the concept of information as a commodity will distort the agendas of institutions . . . . Public interest in the principle of open access must appropriately influence the structure of the information system and its components. It is certain that the information needs of society cannot be defined by the market place alone.

But increasingly this litany of justifications for the state's continued support of the legitimation function in national information policy has come to take on the character of little more than the ritual deployment of slogans and evidences a substantial amount of rhetorical inflation. The reason for this evident corruption of our rhetoric is apparent. For over a decade now the forces of information as a public good have encountered the forces of information as a commodity and lost.

Despite our most valiant efforts we continue to witness a steady change in emphasis in national information policy. Dramatic cuts in federal support for the public sector information delivery system, systematic efforts to "privatize" important aspects of state information dissemination services like the U. S. National Technical Information System, and the across the board attempts by the Office of Management and Budget to curtail sharply government publication programs, have all taken their toll. While American commitment to the principle of free and ready access to information in the form of the nation's library system remains substantial the steady "impoverishment" of the public sector information system continues without pause.

Equally unnerving has been the steady growth of a pro information industry element *within the library profession itself.* Increasingly the profession is finding its official statements on behalf of the public sector delivery of information countered by fellow librarians committed to "information brokerage," "fees for service," and information as a commodity. This unsettling lack of consensus is compounded by the reality that the library profession constitutes a small and relatively impotent force in the contest to influence national information policy and as a result has only limited control over its own future. Louis Vagianos and Barry

Lesser (1990, p. 10) call our attention to the fact that "the age of the library as a standalone depository is at an end" and that

> Much of their future success or failure will depend on the larger environment of the information marketplace, with its changing products, changing actors, and shifting geographical and content boundaries, and the public policy environment, including all levels of government . . . Each will play a major role in defining the framework for adequate answers.

Herbert and Anita Schiller (1988) confirm the current state of affairs when they note that this unfair contest "pits the fundamental principle of American libraries—free access to information—against the interests of the private information suppliers and their advocates in government," and that the battle is raging *inside* and *outside* of libraries where "a combination of forces is weakening the historic principle of free, socially underwritten access" (p. 146).

CONCLUSION

The outcome has been apparent for some time, and the short-term implications for libraries are now clear. First, despite increasingly emotional announcements of the decline of democratic access to information, the government shows little interest in providing the resources necessary to remedy the problems faced by the public sector information system. The conservative ideology now dominant in Washington simply does not promise any return to the glorious 1960s era when libraries were deluged with resources from the federal government. At the same time it appears evident that the state will continue to support private sector initiatives in the information industry, further exacerbating the problems for the nation's public sector library system (NRenaissance Committee, 1994; Office of Technology Assessment, 1994).

This situation promises to further divide the library profession; with the advocates of the library as a "public good" encountering ever stronger resistance from the pro-information industry wing of the profession. Despite the library profession's ability to avoid the awkward self-reflection mandated by Fremont Rider in the mid 1940s, we once again find ourselves facing the prospect of being forced to abandon the cherished goals of the American library system in order to accommodate ourselves to economic exigency and the conservative ideology now governing national communication policy. Thus, librarians find themselves absorbed in intense debates about the very role of the library in American society.

While the future is uncertain (isn't it always?) it would appear clear that many of our current problems are unique, and that historical analogies are not likely to be of great use in solving them. What also seems clear is that we should be cautious of glib formulas for alleviating all our problems, and must somehow find a way to overcome the "dicotomization between those who insist that every piece of data be paid for and those who argue the free use and disbursement of hard-earned information" (Horowitz, 1986, p. 9). Paul Lauter (1991, p. x) reminds us that while it "may seem peculiarly Utopian to challenge the market-oriented thinking of this culture" it is important to keep in mind that "whatever the virtues of a marketplace approach to some areas of human enterprise, the notion that such thinking is appropriate to governing all areas of activity is not only banal but dangerously authoritarian" (see also Kuttner, 1997). When it comes to state intervention in national information policy it has rarely been a question of all or nothing, but rather, as we have repeatedly noted, a matter of emphasis—"ideological" emphasis.

We could do with a good deal less self-righteous rhetoric and a good deal more critical thinking about ways to continue our commitment to democratic principles of dissemination within the context of our growing understanding of the role of the state in fostering free market solutions to societal problems in a democratic/capitalistic society (Vagianos & Lesser, 1990). Somehow we must find a way to transcend constructively this protracted and perilous seesawing of cynical critique and countercritique. Part of our purpose in this book is to contribute to the alleviation of "the profession's lack of inclination to develop a synthetic understanding" because of the "sheer complexity of the issues" (K. Heim, 1986, p. 22). In Chapter 6 of this book we attempt to make our own contribution to this positive, critical rethinking of the role of the librarian, and the mission of the library in the information society. Before we do so, however, we need to examine the central issue of the role of the information professions in the information society.

4

Neutrality, Objectivity, Information Professionals, and Librarians

The fact of the matter is that most of the problems, or at least many of them that we now face, are technical problems .... They are very sophisticated judgements which do not lend themselves to the great sort of "passionate movements" which have stirred this country so often in the past. Now they deal with questions which are beyond the comprehension of most men.

John F. Kennedy

It is quite possible that the new "isms" of tomorrow will be ideologies about knowledge. In tomorrow's intellectual and political philosophies knowledge may well take the central place that property, i.e., things, occupied in capitalism and Marxism.

Peter Drucker

Our thesis is that the twentieth century has continued the transformation, so that the twenty-first will open on a world in which cognitive ability is the decisive dividing force . . . . These channels are increasingly . . . leading to the development of a distinct stratum or social hierarchy, which we hereby dub the Cognitive Elite.

Richard Herrnstein and Charles Murray

INTRODUCTION

The idea that the post-industrial society holds immense promise for the professionalization of those "knowledge workers" who specialize in the creation and deployment of "information" has proven to be an idea of enormous conceptual power in the continuing debate about the implications of the post-industrial society. This dream of professional empowerment has been described as a "narcotic delusion" or a sort of "intellectual smack" that has the power to direct discussions of professionalism into some highly eccentric channels (Luke, 1989). Librarians, too, have seized the notion that their time has finally come and that the post-industrial era marks the concomitant emergence of librarianship as a profession. As Pauline Wilson (1978) noted, the great appeal of Bell's metaphor was that "librarians have usually understood it to mean an enlarged role in society for their profession" (p. 124).

In many ways the idea that librarians will readily qualify as information professionals, or even as *the* information professionals, has been a dominant theme in the library profession's contemplation of the future of library and information services in the post-industrial era. This discussion has too often been carried on without benefit of a clear understanding of how Daniel Bell defined the information professionals, or any real attention to the sociology of professions. As a result much of the discussion surrounding librarians as professionals is shallow, polemical, and generally of little use in understanding the question of professionalization for librarians in the post-industrial era. In what follows we address this problem by first carefully rehearsing Daniel Bell's description of the new information professions. Then we turn to a concise synthesis of the latest research on the sociology of professions in an attempt to evaluate Bell's claim that the information professionals will emerge as the meta-professionals of the post-industrial era. Next we deploy contemporary definitions of the librarian-as-information-professional, and consider the implications of this new "librarian" for the more traditional conceptions of the role of the librarian. Finally, we intend to critically examine the traditional model of the librarian as a neutral and passive public servant in an attempt to illustrate the extent to which this understanding of our traditional mission often masks a more political and cultural underpinning of contemporary library and information service in America. It is our hope that, so armed, the readers of this book will be able to more critically assess the claims and counterclaims of those so passionately engaged in the debate swirling around the notion of librarians as information professionals.

DANIEL BELL DEFINES THE EMERGING
INFORMATION PROFESSIONS

"What is most striking," Daniel Bell wrote in 1977, "is the incredible growth today of the professional class, which is a product of a post-industrial society."

Bell confidently concludes that the "professional class is the largest of its kind in human history" (p. 44). He attributes the rise of the professions, especially the information professions, to the "emergence of a new social framework," a post-industrial society, that constitutes a total break with our past.

"What I am arguing," Bell points out, "is that the major source of structural change in society—the change in the modes of innovation in the relation of science to technology and in public policy—is the change in the character of knowledge: the exponential growth and branching of science, the rise of a new intellectual technology, the creation of systematic research . . . and . . . the codification of theoretical knowledge" (1973a, p. 44).

The central figure in the post-industrial society will be the information professional, for as Bell (1973a, p. 127) insists

> What counts is not raw muscle power, or energy, but information. The central person is the professional, for he is equipped, by his education and training, to provide the kinds of skill that is increasingly demanded in the post-industrial society.

The post-industrial society in its "initial logic" must be a "meritocracy." Bell anticipates that status and income will be based on "technical skill and higher education." Those not possessing the skills necessary to function as information professionals will encounter increasing difficulties in the post-industrial labor market. Bell is cognizant of the problems inherent in the emergence of the new high-status information professions, for, as he notes, "the chief problem of the emerging post-industrial society is the conflict generated by a meritocracy principle which is central to the allocation of position in the knowledge society" (1973a, p. 44).

For Bell the post-industrial society is an "information society" characterized by the emergence of a new professional class of "knowledge workers" or "information professionals." Bell also points out that the high status professionals will be engaged in bringing computers and intellectual technology to bear on the "management of organized complexity," which he views as the central problem of modern society. "Knowledge has of course been necessary in the functioning of any society," Bell (1973a) notes, but "what is distinctive about the post-industrial society is the change in the character of knowledge itself." He goes on to point out that (p. 20):

> What has become decisive for the organization of decisions and the direction of change is the centrality of *theoretical* knowledge—the primacy of theory over empiricism and the codification of knowledge into abstract systems of symbols that, as in any axiomatic system, can be used to illuminate many different and varied areas of experience.

In 1979, Bell outlined the major categories of the "knowledge stratum" or the "information and knowledge sector." In doing so he clearly indicates the stratified nature of the information work force (pp. 182–183):

- The information processors and technical and professional workers. These can be regarded as *occupations*. These are individuals, with some higher education, who handle tasks that require some certified competence.
- The intellectuals and knowledge workers. These are individuals concerned with the creation, evaluation, and, at the research level, transmission and application of knowledge. These are the scientists and scholars, mathematicians and economists, research physicians, and law teachers . . . whose consensus determines which paradigms of knowledge or theories carry greatest weight.
- The creators and critics of culture: novelists, painters.
- The transmitters of culture and knowledge: cultural and intellectual periodicals, museums, publishing houses, libraries, etc.
- The appliers and transmitters of knowledge: engineers.
- Managers and administrators of economic enterprise, public bureaucracies, and nonprofit institutions.
- News and entertainment workers.

Bell (1979, p. 184) suggests that the "knowledge stratum" will be scattered across "four functional estates":

1. Scientific and scholarly;
2. Technological (applied skills);
3. Administrative; and
4. Cultural (artistic and religious).

This, for Bell, constitutes the major contours of the "information and knowledge" occupations. Within this framework, this new "social division of labor," certain information and knowledge occupations will be clearly privileged or "high status," while others will be clearly subordinate. Bell recognized that the emergence of the post-industrial society would dramatically empower science as "a basic institutional necessity of the society" and that this process "by creating and extending a technical intelligencia" would raise "crucial questions about the relation of the technical to the literary intellectual" (1973a, p. 43). This issue, which is a central cause of tension in the library profession, has been analyzed from a number of perspectives in preceding chapters, but it remains for us here to examine the way in which Bell thinks science will be empowered. Here we must confront Bell's difficult, and controversial, idea of "intellectual technology."

For Bell, the "major intellectual and sociological problems of the post-industrial society" are those of the rational management of "large-scale systems" or "organized complexity." Bell (1973a, p. 28) feels that this pressing task will be undertaken by means of a new "intellectual technology":

One can say that the methodological premise of the second half of the twentieth century is the management of organized complexity (the complexity of large organizations and systems, the complexity of theory with a large number of variables), the identification and implementation of strategies for rational choice in games against nature and games between persons, and the development of a new intellectual technology which, by the end of the century, may be as salient in human affairs as machine technology has been for the past century and a half.

This slippery, but vital, concept seems to connote a combination of software (i.e., artificial intelligence and expert systems) and the computer. "What has become decisive for the organization of decisions and the direction of change is the centrality of *theoretical* knowledge," Bell insists, the "primacy of theory over empiricism and the codification of knowledge into abstract systems of symbols that, as in any axiomatic system, can be used to illuminate many different and varied areas of experience" (1973a, p. 20).

Bell is quite explicit in indicating the characteristics of the new intellectual technology. Noting that since 1940 we have seen a remarkable growth "of new fields" dedicated to solving the problems associated with large-scale systems, he lists them as "information theory, cybernetics, decision theory, game theory, utility theory, stochastic processes . . . sophisticated set theory" (1973a, p. 29). In short, Bell (1973a, pp. 29–30) notes "an *intellectual* technology is the substitution of algorithms (problem-solving rules) for intuitive judgements":

These algorithms may be embodied in an automatic machine or a computer program or a set of instructions based on some statistical or mathematical formula; the statistical and logical techniques that are used in dealing with "organized complexity" are efforts to formalize a set of decision rules.

"What is distinctive about the new intellectual technology," Bell (1973a) notes, "is its effort to define rational action and to identify the means of achieving it" (p. 30). Bell also pointedly concludes that "the goal of the new intellectual technology is, neither more nor less . . . the dream of 'ordering' the mass society." He concisely states that if "the computer is the tool, then decision theory is its master." The object, of course, is to establish a special "compass of rationality: the 'best' solution to the choices perplexing men" (p. 33).

What should now be apparent, after this reprise of Bell, is that the high status information professionals in the post-industrial society will be the makers and controllers of the new intellectual (i.e., decisionmaking) technology. "The 'new men' are the scientists, the mathematicians, the economists, and the engineers of the new intellectual technology," Bell (1973a, p. 344) insists. It is in this sense that he can conclude in the foreward to the 1976 edition of *The Coming of Post-Industrial Society* that, "in effect, what a post-industrial transformation means is the enhancement of instrumental powers, powers over nature, and powers, even, over people" (p. xxi).

Bell endorses a longheld liberal insistence that professionals should be "objective" and "detached" but that they must not be passive. Knowledge driven actions are seen as "merely impersonal technically necessary reactions" designed to solve problems central to the smooth operation of the society.

For Bell, the intellectual technology of the post-industrial era becomes the new logos, the principle around which all other societal relations will be organized. Jon Wagner (1979) has called it a "meta-technology," which he defines as "technologies for the development of technology" (p. 730). Judith A. Perrolle (1991, p. 221) argues that Bell's intellectual technology might better be defined as "knowledge engineering":

> Knowledge engineering includes efforts to organize intellectual activity into a set of computer-coordinated tasks by means of data management and decision-support systems . . . . It also involves attempts to mechanize actual decision-making and knowledge production activities using expert systems, and other types of artificial intelligence software.

She notes that in the post-industrial framework "information itself" is seen as *the* commodity that will be produced and sold on the information marketplace and that "information can be produced by the computer in the same way that products were made by the factory machinery of the first industrial revolution . . ." (p. 225). Timothy Luke (1989) interprets Bell's intellectual technology as reflecting the "essential bias" of the post-industrial era: "the creation of new social formations tied to the exchange-driven production, distribution, consumption, interpretation, and reproduction of information" (p. 11).

And then in the 1990s we encounter the controvertial work of Herrnstein and Murray (1994), which begins with a suggestion that could have been drawn almost verbatim from Bell's 1973 book (p.25):

> Our thesis is that the twentieth century has continued the transformation, so that the twenty-first will open on a world in which cognitive ability is the decisive dividing force. The shift is more subtle than the previous one but more momentous. Social Class remains the vehicle of social life, but intelligence now pulls the train . . . . leading to the development of a cognitive stratum, which we hereby dub the cognitive elite.

"Cognitive elite," "New Class," "Knowledge Elite," "Information Professionals": It all seems to add up to the same thing. We are witnessing the emergence of an information society where the class system will be dictated by (and reflected in) "cognitive stratification." But the differences in the *Coming of Post-Industrial Society* and *The Bell Curve* are also quite striking (Harris, 1996). Where Bell predicted the rise of a meritocratic knowledge elite he never explicitly predicted who would win and who would loose. Herrnstein and Murray, on the other hand, explicitly name the winners and losers, and indicate that the cognitively weak, who appear to them to be mainly African-Americans and women of all races, will be destined to operate at the margins of the society, outside the information economy where the winners will all reside. It was, of course, the *explicit* naming of names that generated the massive reaction to *The Bell Curve*, and opened the authors to charges of racism, sexism, and elitism (Fraser, 1995; Jacoby & Glauberman, 1995). Perhaps the best way to highlight the implications of the latest incarnation of Bell's "meritocracy" is with the riveting and troubling words of Kathryn Marie Dudley (1994, p. 177):

> In the ritual symbolism of postindustrial society, industrial workers have become the new American primitive. They are the people who work with their hands in a society that increasingly values work done with the mind. Their social distance from the new cultural ideal is measured and legitimated by educational credentials. If they wish to survive in the modern age and claim a place in the middle class, it is said, they will have to educate themselves to do the kind of work demanded of people living in a postindustrial society. The kind of social change required is clearly unidirectional: blue-collar workers must adapt . . . The nation's industrial past plays no part in our vision of the future.

The controversial nature of Bell's conception of the information professions should now be clear. While he concludes that there will be substantial variety among the "knowledge stratum" he nevertheless seems to privilege scientific over cultural knowledge workers, and he clearly indicates that the information professions will be stratified, where those professionals engaged in the construction and application of the new intellectual technology for rational decisionmaking in the production of information-as-a-commodity will reign as the high status professionals or "meta-professionals" of the post-industrial era. A consideration of the implications of this scenario for the librarian's quest for professional status must be delayed momentarily while we consider the way in which sociologists of the professions have received Bell's vision of the professional future.

THE VERY IDEA OF AN "INFORMATION PROFESSION": THE SOCIOLOGY OF PROFESSIONAL DEVELOPMENT

Marie R. Haug (1977) notices the variety with which sociologists have viewed the notion of a profession. She also points out that a common thread linking all of these views of professionalism is that "knowledge monopoly forms the basis of professional power" and this combined with "varying claims to an altruistic orientation" is what provides the professional with autonomy and "institutionalizes client obligations to trust the professional and comply with his prescriptions" (p. 217). This "competence gap," leads society to believe that "professionals have the right to define the client's problem, outline the necessary course of action to deal with the problem, and manage or supervise compliance with the action plan, because they and only they in their occupational roles know what is in that client's best interest" (p. 217).

Sociologists of the professions appear to agree on this general understanding of the "profession" and also agree that "autonomy" and "power to prescribe" based on "exclusive cognitive competence" are essential ingredients in the making of the "high status" professions (for general treatments see Abbott, 1988; Brint, 1994; Friedson, 1986, 1994; Sullivan, 1995). Most also agree with Harold Wilensky (1964) who suggests that the uncritical idea that everybody will be a professional in the post-industrial era is a "bit of sociological romance," and that in reality "very few occupations will achieve the authority of the established professions" and the tendency to call all occupations "professions" only obscures "the newer structural forms now emerging" (p. 137). Given our special interest in the potential emergence of a meta-profession of knowledge workers, it is necessary for us to explore more critically and systematically what we know about the emergence of the high status professions in an attempt to assess Daniel Bell's claim that information professionals will achieve that status in the post-industrial era.

The sociology of the professions has undergone several significant revisions over the past several decades. Originally, sociologists felt that one could best understand professions, and the professional project, by attending to the "traits" of professions. This approach led sociologists to define professions as those occupations which society willingly grants "special power and prestige" because these occupations have "special competence in esoteric bodies of knowledge linked to central needs and values of the social system, and because professions are devoted to the service of the public, above and beyond material incentives" (Larson, 1977, p. x). Larson refers to this definition as the "ideal-typical" model, and notes that it is inevitably followed by a list of special attributes of the "real professions," that is, medicine and law. What becomes apparent is that such a model assumes that prestige and autonomy flow naturally from the cognitive and normative bases of professional work. At this point we need to note briefly the extent to which this model corresponds to Daniel Bell's understanding of the rise of the information professions: Their enhanced status and power will flow naturally from their cognitive base—their command of the new intellectual technology—and their commitment to public service.

What emerges from this model is a uncritical picture which emphasizes the characteristics of the high status professions, like medicine and law. That is, students of the professions analyze the characteristics of the professions and then conclude that would-be professionals need only mimic the high status professions if they desire professional status. The practical effect of all this has been that occupations, like librarianship, spend inordinate amounts of time trying to fit the ideal-typical profile so that they may magically be transmuted into professions.

Thus, the ideal-typical model tends to govern our understanding of how professions are made. As a result, we find that the pages of our professional literature are full of lists of characteristics of professions, followed by suggestions that if we will only strengthen one or another of these characteristics we too can be professionals. While the lists vary, most would contain the following characteristics:

- Prolonged specialized training;
- A body of theoretical knowledge;
- A strong and cohesive professional association;
- A strong service orientation; and
- An enforceable professional code of ethics.

   Contemporary sociologists of the professions have become increasingly dissatisfied with this framework for analyzing the professions. They insist that the ideal-typical model tends to actually mask the way in which occupations really gain professional status and in many ways has become an ideology capable of systematically undermining our ability to understand the true nature of the professional project. Magali Larson (1977) insists that what is masked is the intensely *political* nature of the professional project. She claims that in this way the ideal-typical model renders the question of professional *power* unproblematic.

   What Larson and others are now arguing is that the stages in the successful completion of the professional project must be seen in a decidedly political context. Reconceived in this way the stages in professionalism would unfold as follows. First, the elite leadership of a would-be profession must successfully "negotiate the boundaries of an area in the social division of labor" (Larson, 1977, p. xii). This "negotiation" involves both an internal and external component. Internally, the professional leadership must forcefully strive for the codification of an esoteric body of knowledge and the development of a professional paradigm (Larson, 1977, pp. 40–41).

   The other aspect of this initial step is jurisdictional. As Andrew Abbott (1988, p. 2) points out, "jurisdictional boundaries are perpetually in dispute, both in local practice and in national claims," and he argues (p. 33) that

> Each profession is bound to a set of tasks by ties of jurisdiction, the strengths and weaknesses of these ties being established in the processes of actual professional work. Since none of these links is absolute or permanent, the professions make up an interacting system, an ecology. Professions compete within this system, and a profession's success reflects as much the situations of its competitors and the system structure as it does the profession's own efforts. From time to time, tasks are created, abolished, or reshaped by external forces, with consequent jostling and readjustment within the system of professions.

   In short, the nascent profession must be united in and around an exclusive cognitive base, a uniform professional commodity, and jurisdictional conflicts with other professional contenders must be resolved.

   The external component is that part of the professional project which utilizes persuasion directed outside of the profession, "that is, to the relevant elites, the potential public or publics, and the political authorities" (Larson, 1977, p. xii). Ultimately, the would-be profession must convince the state to offer it certain powers in exchange for professional service in the community's best interests. What the state must provide is the foundation for a "monopoly of knowledge." This monopolistic environment can most effectively be created through state intervention which provides the profession with the right to

- Control the production of the producers. That is, the state must grant the profession the right to designate the credentials necessary for the legal practice of the profession and allow for the imposition of criminal sanctions on those who attempt to violate the professional monopoly. This state-endorsed monopoly allows professionals to create favorable conditions of supply and demand for professional services.
- Second, the state must grant the profession the right to "define the standards by which its superior competence is to be judged." This state granted autonomy "allows the experts to select almost at will the inputs they will receive from" the lay public (Larson, 1977, p. xiii). "The central characteristic of expert intellectual work," Larson (1977) argues, "is that it cannot be established from the outside *that a given result should be obtained in a given time.*" And she notes, this power is linked to the professionals' state-aided monopoly of knowledge (p. 235).

In short, the key to the professional project is the deliberate establishment of a state-endorsed monopoly over "esoteric bodies of knowledge linked to central needs and values of the social system" (Larson, 1977, p. x). What should now be apparent is that the emergence of a profession is anything but *natural.*

Given this understanding of the nature of the high status professions what can we make of Daniel Bell's suggestion that we will witness the emergence of an "information profession" in the post-industrial era? At least in theory, he could be correct. Recall that Bell has suggested that the management of "organized complexity" constitutes the most vital of tasks in the post-industrial era. Remember that he insists that the key to the management of this vital social problem will be the construction of an "intellectual technology," which will be deployed in the service of the society at large. Remember also that he argues that this new intellectual technology will be created, controlled, and deployed by a professional class "the new men"—who will emerge as the high status information professionals.

If information-as-commodity and "intellectual technology" become the driving forces in both the economy and the solution of societal problems, then it is conceivable that a new meta-profession of "information professionals" could evolve in the post-industrial era. The disparate occupations which would be unified under the heading of "information professional" could indeed be granted "special power and prestige" due to their "special competence in esoteric bodies of knowledge linked to central needs and values of the social system" (Larson, 1977, p. x).

Andrew Abbott (1988), who has reflected indepth on this question, concludes that to-date, "no coherent set of people has in fact emerged to take jurisdiction in this area" (p. 245). While he is skeptical that this will ever happen, he deploys a systems model to suggest how it *might happen*. Abbott (p. 215) sees a recurrent theme in the history of professional development:

> A characteristic story in the system of professions begins with a disturbance—a new technology requiring professional judgement or a new technique for old professional work. These disturbances undermine the balance between work and professions and lead to a variety of readjustments. Eventually the various parts of the system absorb the disturbance and balance returns.

Abbott also notes the intense interdependence of the professions, and the extent to which professions must compete (engage in jurisdictional disputes), both within and outside of the profession once a system disturbance, like the rise of the new "intellectual technology," is felt.

These jurisdictional disputes, which are clearly in evidence within and among the information professions today, will create an environment where "tasks are created, abolished, or reshaped by external forces, with consequent jostling and readjustment within the system of professions" (p. 33). "On this analysis," Abbott argues, "there are three general stages in a system-based historical description: disturbances, jurisdictional contests, and the transformations leading to balance" (p. 215). Anyone observing the current situation would be led to conclude that we have witnessed the system disturbance in the form of Bell's "intellectual technology" and that we are currently in the midst of the jurisdictional contests which are focused on the codification of knowledge and the development of a dominant professional paradigm. The victors in this professional project will earn the right to define the "information profession" and monopolize the creation and deployment of the post-industrial "intellectual technology."

WHERE DO LIBRARIANS FIT IN? A NOTE ON THE SOCIOLOGY OF LIBRARIANSHIP

Librarians have long exhibited a curious, and intense, status anxiety that is reflected in endless polemics about the professional status (or lack thereof) among librarians (Pauline Wilson, 1982). Most of that literature is of little use to us here where our concern has to be with rigorous and critical analysis of the professional status of librarians within the context of the sociology of the professions outlined above. What we must briefly attend to are the few serious attempts to assess the professional status of librarians as a preliminary to examining the implications of Daniel Bell's conception of the information professions for the library profession in the post-industrial era. While these portrayals of the library profession are not particularly flattering they must nevertheless be confronted before we move on.

What is readily apparent as we examine the literature on the library profession is that all serious students of the subject notice that the library, and the librarian, are firmly situated in what Daniel Bell defines as the subordinate "cultural" realm in the post-industrial society. As one scholar notes, "this social function of expanding the collective memory places librarianship at the center of cultural transmission" (Winter, 1988, p. 81). J. G. Meijer (1982, p. 26) concluded, after a thorough canvas of the literature on librarianship, that

> Librarianship is a form of cultural enterprise whose main characteristic is the stimulation of the optimum use of mankind's cultural heritage insofar as it consists of coded thoughts recorded in documents that are and must be held in readiness for use with the ultimate objective of making possible cultural progress.

Patrick Williams and Joan Pearce (1978) agreed when they argued that "the preservation of social and cultural forms, of knowledge and human experience, depend on the preservation of literature." "The library performs the critical function of preservation," they concluded, "which is the keystone of civilization" (p. 95).

Other studies have demonstrated the extent to which librarians have been subordinate to the culture producers within the cultural realm. Librarians are seen as passive members of an occupation best viewed as "mere handmaidens to other cultural agents" (Butler, 1951, p. 246). This lack of professional authority and exclusive cognitive power has meant that the librarian is seen essentially "as a gatekeeper and custodian of the 'stock room'" (Goode, 1962, p. 15).

Patrick Wilson (1977, pp. 101–102) argues that this passive and "unprofessional stance" leads one to the conclusion that librarians are not professionals and that this is evident in the character of library information service:

> The librarian undertakes to answer questions insofar as direct answers can be discovered in standard sources; the librarian does not undertake to engage in computations, analyses and criticism of sources, evaluation, interpretation, inference, synthesis, application of information to particular problems.

"Avoiding responsibility," Wilson argues, "means avoiding professionalism" and the superficial bibliographical services provided by librarians "rest on shallow and undependable use of standard reference works to answer a limited category of questions" (p. 104, 108).

All of these characteristics add up to a rejection of the idea that traditional librarianship is or could be considered a profession. William Joseph Reeves (1980, p. 7) concluded that

The occupation is unable to determine who can and cannot practice as a librarian; it controls neither access into the occupation through the formal avenues of socialization nor entry into positions of employment.

William Goode (1962, p. 18) drew similar conclusions when he noted that

The librarian is a gatekeeper who can exclude almost no one; a guardian who can protect primarily against vandals and thieves; a stockroom custodian who must hand over any of his stock even if he is sure the person really wants or needs something else.

Andrew Abbott (1988) notes that while this picture of the librarian might be viewed as unflattering, it nevertheless reflects reality and is founded on the fact that since librarians have faced little competition as guardians of the cultural heritage in print form, "librarians had no real incentive for structural change other than a general desire for social repute" (p. 222). That is, since librarians "faced little competition in their own area" they felt no real pressure to "invade other areas."

But all of that was to change with the emergence of the post-industrial era. Leigh Estabrook (1989) sets the stage for the next section of this chapter when she notes that librarians are facing a unique and aggressive invasion of their turf "in library and information services." This new competition will force structural change, and librarians are being forced into a battle for "status and territory." Estabrook sounds what has become a recurrent battle cry when she concludes that "not to compete, or not consciously to seek growth, may lead to a profound loss" (p. 295). Mary Lee Bundy and Paul Wasserman (1968, p. 25) drew this conclusion even earlier when they argued that

The conditions of modern times . . . are such that if librarianship does not move much more rapidly forward toward enhanced professionalism, the field will not only decline rapidly, but ultimately will face obsolescence.

The goal, they insist, must be to "forge a new professional identity" (p. 26). It is now time to address the many faceted attempt on the part of a diverse group of library leaders to forge a new identity for the librarian in response to the emergence of the information professions in the post-industrial era.

LIBRARIANS AS INFORMATION PROFESSIONALS: THE ATTEMPT TO FORGE A NEW PROFESSIONAL IDENTITY

In our examination of the library profession's confrontation with the implications of the post-industrial era, it is important to briefly reflect on an earlier moment in library history. That time, the period of the Great Society, the Kennedy and

Johnson administrations, was a period when the nation was swept with a reformist spirit decidedly tilted toward the legitimation function of government as outlined in Chapter 3. Librarians, like other public servants, were smitten with the same reformist urge, and they set about trying to find ways to create a niche in the welfare-oriented focus of the larger society (Bundy & Stielow, 1987).

A new breed of activists emerged and insisted that the library profession had an opportunity to contribute significantly to the progressive reform abroad in the land, while at the same time enhancing their status as professionals. Perhaps the most aggressive and influential of the new breed was Paul Wasserman, the Dean of the Library School at the University of Maryland, and the author of *The New Librarianship: A Challenge for Change* (1972), which was published just as the movement began to wane. Advocating the notion of the librarian as "change agent" Wasserman attacked traditional librarianship for its "bookish orientation," its "elite values," and its "institutional" focus.

This traditional emphasis on high culture in printed form made the library of little interest to aggressive change agents and instead appealed mainly to women "from a thin stratum of relatively high-status social classes, individuals from backgrounds in the humanities" who share a fundamental commitment to the "transcendent cultural values of books and reading" (pp. 249, 247). Wasserman quoted a library school student on this matter (pp. 247–248):

> Those of us who hold the traditional middle class view of libraries as quiet depositories of books and periodicals . . . find the concept of libraries as active disseminators of information not only hard to accept, but rather repugnant . . . . I kind of like traditional libraries—at least the good ones and much prefer the book oriented system.

The late Oliver Garceau (1949, pp. 50–51) put it quite clearly when he noted that the "Library Faith" was founded upon the

> fundemental belief, so generally accepted as to be often left unsaid, in the virtue of the printed word, the reading of which is good in itself, and upon the preservation of which many basic values in our civilization rest.

This value system, Wasserman insisted, led librarians to focus an inordinate amount of attention on the collection, preservation, and protection of what Kathleen Molz (1966-1967) nicely labeled the "High Pornography." Wasserman (1972, p. 242) attacked the very credo of the profession when he insisted that the library profession's obsession with intellectual freedom represented a "spurious issue" that

> serves to deflect attention from the more central question of the library's responsibility to foster a climate and render full access to information in all the ways which it holds the resources to achieve. For the genuine issue in the culture is not whether

individuals have free access to suggestive prose, but whether they have access to the intelligence to aid them to improve their social, political, and economic condition.

It hardly seems necessary to remind our readers that "them" represented the lower classes.

This passive and misguided dedication to the collection and preservation of high culture in printed form, Wasserman argued, obstructed the professional project of librarians, and rendered the library a repressive support for the status quo. "The strategic element which has been lacking," he noted, "has been a reconstructed ideological base for librarianship which might transform it from what it is and what it has been—an institution concentrated upon collections and procedures—to a client system" (p. 251). What he was advocating was advocacy—advocacy for the poor and disadvantaged—"a client response system" based on a social work model (p. 265).

What Wasserman and others were able to glimpse was the extent to which the library was an institution embedded in the cultural realm of society, and the extent to which its structural and functional characteristics were determined by its definition as an institution contrived to consume, preserve, transmit, and reproduce high culture in printed form (Harris, 1986a). They also recognized the extent to which this institutional "ideology" dictated the character and role of librarians, and the very nature of the library's audience itself.

What Wasserman and other "change agents" failed to understand was the enormous power of the cultural definition of the library—what Michael Winter (1988) has called the "overwhelming counterweight of historical tradition." Winter (pp. 78–79) noted that facile calls for abrupt system change overlook a fundamental reality:

> Even if libraries disappeared tomorrow, they would at that point have existed for many thousands of years, and for that reason alone would exert a great influence on social and cultural life for centuries afterward . . . . So for the present, the foreseeable future, and for an immense stretch of the past, libraries appear to be very durable institutions.

Michael Buckland (1988, p. 208) emphasized this fact while struggling to resist mentioning the word book:

> Libraries and librarians deal with physical objects, with *representations* of knowledge, culture, information, facts, and beliefs. Libraries deal with texts and images—or, more strictly, with text-bearing objects and image-bearing objects, with millions of these objects on miles of shelving.

In short, libraries are collections of books, and librarians are the keepers of the books (Harris, 1995; Harris & Hannah, 1996).

The power of the cultural mission of the library to dictate the nature of library services and the characteristics of librarians themselves is nicely encapsulated in the proceedings of a symposium held in 1964 on the occasion of the *Wilson Library Bulletin*'s fiftieth anniversary. The symposium was dedicated to a discussion of the "library of the future" and included such professional voices as Jesse Shera, Lester Asheim, Carolyn Whitenack, Emerson Greenaway, and William Shepard Dix. At one point Dix, one of the profession's most respected "scholar librarians," confidently articulated his view that the role of the library was to make available serious books to serious readers. He calmly argued that "this may seem old-fashioned, but an attractive room and a wide-ranging collection of books, freely accessible, seems to me what a library is." At that point Whitenack sharply criticized Dix's conservative view that libraries should serve only the literate elite, and insisted it was time for libraries to assume the responsibility of serving "all people." At which point Dix admitted that he might be "tied too closely to the library as a collection of books" but that nevertheless the information needs of "undereducated people" were not the legitimate concern of libraries. At the end of the symposium, Dix confirmed what were to prove Wasserman's worst fears when he noted that the "intellectual needs of a wide portion of the public" could be well met outside the library. While he felt some hybrid organization might emerge to meet their needs, he still maintained that libraries must remain "identified by name with books" and that librarians must rededicate themselves to the high culture mission of the library (quoted in Harris & Tourjee, 1983, p. 58).

That the power of the library's high cultural mission was capable of overwhelming the advocates of the "librarian as change agent" is now apparent to serious historians. That fact, however, was not so clear to a new generation of librarians who once again saw an opportunity to transcend the institutional restraints on their cherished professional project and set out on an aggressive campaign to articulate and deploy a new professional paradigm which portrayed librarians as "information professionals."

THE RISE OF THE INFORMATION PARADIGM: F. W. LANCASTER AND "FUTURE LIBRARIANSHIP"

In 1983, F. W. Lancaster published a paper entitled "Future Librarianship: Preparing for an Unconventional Career." In that essay he quickly pointed to the extent to which "librarianship is the most institutionalized of professions." Lancaster then suggested that the reason for the consistent privileging of library over librarian is an "historical accident," that is, "libraries existed before librarians did" (p. 747). Despite this historical accident, what Michael Winter (1988) would call the "overwhelming counterweight of historical tradition," Lancaster wondered why contemporary librarians still "seem to concentrate on a physical facility—a building that houses artifacts—rather than on the technical expertise of skilled practitioners, which is surely the most important thing the profession has to offer" (p. 747).

Arguing that such "misguided emphases" explained our unflattering image and lack of status, Lancaster called for renewed attention to the professional project in the context of the post-industrial society. Drawing an analogy between librarianship and medicine Lancaster insisted that librarians must become "deinstitutionalized" if they were to play a leadership role among the information professions. He also insisted that librarians really have no choice, since the emergence of the computer and telecommunications advances dictated the end of the book and its warehouse. He casually concluded that "I see little future for the library" (p. 750).

But what of the librarian? Here Lancaster is more sanguine. "It seems possible," he notes, "that the librarian could long outlive the library." For as he points out, "in an age of information, information specialists may increase rather than decline in value." Or, to put it another way, "in an age of electronics we may need 'electronic librarians'" (p. 750). Aware of Bell's notion of a meta-profession of knowledge workers Lancaster concludes that (p. 750):

> Because the collection, processing, and dissemination of information is such an essential element in our lives, librarians, as skilled information providers, could gain considerably in both value and recognition.

To do so librarians will need to move outside the walls of the "crumbling" institutional setting, and into the marketplace, where they will become "freelance librarians," "information brokers," or members of "group practices somewhat resembling present group practices in medicine and law" (Lancaster, 1982a, pp. 150–152). While Lancaster suggests that this "electronic librarian" will abandon all of the old tasks of the traditional librarian in the institutional setting, such as book selection, cataloging, and management, he offers little help in defining exactly what the electronic librarian will do. He does suggest that librarians of the post-industrial era must possess more advanced specialized subject knowledge than is currently the case. He also notes the need for sophisticated database access skills, and perhaps they will need to develop advanced "information analysis" abilities (1983, p. 750):

> searching, selecting the best of the information retrieved, and submitting the evaluated results to the requester. The information specialist then, is essentially an information consultant.

These brief suggestions only remotely reflect Daniel Bell's much more rigorous definition of the characteristics of the meta-professionals in the post-industrial era, and one is left with the sense that Lancaster's blueprint is incomplete (Larsen, 1988). But, we should quickly note, there was no shortage of other proponents of more detailed guidelines for the design and production of electronic librarians.

Perhaps the most detailed and disturbing analysis of the new information professionals was presented by Patrick Wilson in a relentlessly critical essay entitled "Public Knowledge, Private Ignorance" (1977). Concluding that contemporary librarianship represented a decidedly "unprofessional" approach to information service Wilson set out to define the information professions within the context of Bell's notion of "intellectual technology." Noting that "the best and indeed the only practical way of making large bodies of specialized knowledge available to most people is by making available the services of expert, knowledgeable advisors," Wilson continues (p. 124)

> The social division of labor in the production and utilization of knowledge both encourages the development of an ever more remote supply of knowledge and provides a way of partially overcoming that remoteness because it both leads to the concentration of knowledge in various occupational specialties and makes the increasing stock of knowledge available in the persons of the specialists.

Wilson envisions the emergence of a number of groupings of meta-professionals in the post-industrial era, and notes that the job description of the members of "such a new profession does not look like a simple extension of the present practice of librarianship" (p. 117). He suggests that two broad groupings of occupations will emerge under the heading "information system specialists." The first, and most powerful, he chooses to call the "decision technologist" and this is the information professional who will design and control Bell's "intellectual technology." Developing and deploying Bell's intellectual technology the decision technologists will be engaged in the creation of a "normative technology of information" which he defines as (p. 118)

> a technology of the choice of the best patterns of information gathering and information use . . . . The best patterns of information gathering would be specified by reference to uses to be made, and specifying use would be specifying, entirely or in part, the decision procedures to be followed.

A second major category of information professional would be what Wilson labels the "information doctors." Information doctors, like decision technologists, aim at "making prescriptions." Wilson notes that this group of information professionals will have less professional power because unlike the decision technologists they do not tell the client how he should behave, but rather "simply" try "to predict that, if a particular sort of information system . . . is used, decisions will improve" (p. 118). Wilson notes that neither of these occupational categories are well developed, and he is less optimistic than Lancaster when he concludes that "neither seems likely to practice in a library setting" (p. 119).

What Wilson provides is an intensely realistic, but not cynical, assessment of the library profession within the context of Bell's notion of the emerging information profession. In doing so he reminds librarians that the transition to full professional status in the post-industrial era will not be effortless (as some professional cheerleaders have suggested) and most importantly, that it will demand a dramatically different kind of training, professional ideology, and competitive spirit, if the professional aspirations of librarians are to bear fruit in the post-industrial era.

While librarians may not want to hear too realistic a description of the likely characteristics of the new information professionals, they nevertheless have been offered repeated doses of rhetoric designed to alert them to the daunting task that lies before them if they want to launch a genuine campaign for admission to the high status information professions. Richard O. Mason (1990) made some aspects of this task crystal clear when he noted that: "Information professionals deal with information in an objective form, rather than in a subjective form. That is, they are involved fundamentally with technology" (p. 125). He also forcefully insists that the central feature of professional status is a "power asymmetry" between the client and the professional. He points out that the information professional will bring his control of "rational, technical knowledge" and technology to bear in order to produce a "desired effect" for the client (p. 126).

All of these authors argue—correctly, we think—that the high status information professions will be dominated by those who possess the scientific skills necessary to create the intellectual technology, and the power to control its use in the private marketplace. The meta-professionals will deploy their power over the new intellectual technology to resolve the complex problems facing mass society. Seen in this light we can now appreciate the extent to which the advocates of the librarian-as-information-professional are calling for a fundamental ideological break with our past (Harris & Hannah, 1992). The advocates of the librarian-as-information-professional see themselves as the carriers of historical progress, and it should come as no surprise that the advocates of traditional values in librarianship are portrayed as the misguided defenders of a dying socio/economic order. The advocates of the information revolution see themselves as the architects of a new professional era responsible for slaying outmoded professional ideologies and institutional practices and creating the revolutionary future where librarians will take their rightful place among the meta-information professionals of the post-industrial era.

Some of the carriers of this revolutionary ideal are quite precise in delineating the extent and nature of the changes required if librarians are to negotiate successfully their way to the top of the emerging information profession. Others offer only glib and unrealistic rhetoric designed to reassure or provoke the profession. It should be clear from the forgoing analysis that the library profession will have to undergo a dramatic and painful ideological and structural metamorphosis if it hopes to position itself at the top of the emerging high status information professions. The traditional role and charter of the library and library profession "has been made obsolete," Daniel H. Carter (1981) insists, "we can no longer stand on traditional policies, practices and services. We must change!" (p. 1386). Librarians are being urged to say their "final farewells to the book" and the cherished high culture ethic of the "book people."

Furthermore, they are being encouraged to dedicate themselves to a market driven sense of the value of knowledge and information, and significantly qualify their absolutist stance on intellectual freedom. As Derber, Schwartz, and Magrass (1990) point out, the new information professionals will have to come to grips with a fundamental contradiction. For the very foundation of professionalism is exclusive cognitive control of expertise, that is, "to make knowledge their private property" and to prevent its "spread throughout the population." This "schizoid dilemma" between the notion of "open communication" and "knowledge as property" must be confronted by all would-be information professionals. Roma Harris (1993, p. 875) made the same point for librarians when she noted that "the pursuit of the type of professionalism exhibited in the male fields is basically incompatible with the equitable sharing of resourses," so characteristic of library service.

We can summarize some other apparent changes as follows:

- Library recruits would have to be drawn from the sciences rather than the humanities. The cultural role of libraries would have to be replaced with an emphasis on science and technology.
- Librarians would have to abandon their passive neutrality and adopt a much more authoritative and prescriptive stance toward their clients, and in doing so would need to adopt a much more rigorous definition of adequate professional performance and liability. Fundamentally this would mean that librarians would have to abandon the longstanding belief that they must avoid trying to "influence the user's opinions" (Wagers, 1978, p. 268).
- Librarians would have to abandon the notion of information as a public good and adopt a entrepreneurial model of information as a commodity which could dictate an emphasis on the information needs of affluent elite clienteles, and a "separation from lower status groups" (Estabrook, 1989, p. 295).
- Librarians would have to abandon their commitment to the book as artifact and widely embrace the electronic revolution.
- Librarians would have to abandon traditional practice and master the new intellectual technology.
- Librarians would have to abandon their cherished emphasis on broadbased general knowledge as the foundation of professional practice and accept the need for advanced and highly specialized technical training.
- Librarians would have to face the reality that a female-intensive occupation would need to alter its gender characteristics in the transition to the status of an information profession. Historically, the promotion of an occupation to the status of profession has been accompanied by male domination of the profession, both in numbers and leadership (this last point, the effort of the aspiring information profession to "escape its female identity" (R. Harris, 1992), and

the implications of such an attempt, deserves extended coverage and will be treated as a separate and key issue in the next chapter).

Broadly defined these ideological and structural changes have come to represent a new professional identity defined by Apostle and Raymond (1986, p. 378) as the "information paradigm":

> An aim of those who advance this information model is to convince librarians that they must abandon their old self-perception as custodians of books and enter into the new world of information . . . . Information professionals are people whose work is focused on the processing of information, is frequently external to the library, is often freelance, who sell their services to a well-defined segmented market and who are highly dependent on electronic technology.

They also make clear the extent to which this new model for exclusive cognitive competence contradicts longstanding principle and practice in traditional librarianship. What appears to be happening in contemporary library and information science is that we are witnessing what sociologists of the professions label a classic "jurisdictional" battle directed at the negotiation of an area in the social division of labor.

Abbott (1988) points out that these "jurisdictional boundaries are perpetually in dispute" and that we are currently witnessing a struggle within and between professional groups for dominance in the information marketplace. He also points out that inevitably these "system disturbances" will be resolved, but not without a fight, and that we are likely to witness substantial abolition, creation, and reshaping of professional tasks and boundaries before the system "absorbs the disturbance and balance returns" (p. 215). Thus, librarians should not find the current level of debate surprising, for what is at stake is the very nature of professional work, that is, librarians and other information professionals are engaged in a jurisdictional dispute focused on the job descriptions of librarians in the post-industrial era.

Nor is it of much use to suggest that we are uninterested in the heated and often tedious debates that so heavily freight the pages of our professional literature. For as many sociologists of the professions have noted, the system of professions is a sort of "ecology" with each professional specialty linked to each other professional specialty in a tension laden interdependence. As a result a system disturbance like the emergence of the post-industrial era will generate intense jurisdictional disputes that simply cannot be ignored by professionals embedded in the system. Thus, in a very real sense, librarians *must* engage in this effort to define the nature of library and information service in the context of the changed conditions of the post-industrial era, or face continued erosion of their professional status or even complete "deprofessionalization" of the field (Nielsen, 1980).

This situation is further complicated by the fact that the conventional defense of professional neutrality that forms the bedrock of the library profession's credo would now appear to be bankrupt. That is, the argument that librarians are simply the neutral guardians of the transcendent values of books and reading—"the key-stone of civilization"—has been widely challenged by recent work (Buschman and Carbone, 1991; M. H. Harris, 1986a, 1995; Harris & Itoga, 1991). We now possess a better understanding of the extent to which the library is an institution embedded in a stratified ensemble of institutions functioning in the high cultural region, an ensemble of institutions dedicated to the creation, transmission, and production of the hegemonic ideology (M. H. Harris 1986a).

This new understanding of the "traditional" library challenges the "apolitical" conception of the library so commonly held by library professionals, and strips the library of the ethical and political innocence attributed to it by library apologists. It is now harder to justify the naive idea that books and libraries simply reflect the best that has been thought and written in Western society. We are, instead, forced to face the fact that libraries and their contents have always been linked "to the power and privilege of certain classes to represent the world through books in ways that serve their interests" (Carey, 1984, p. 108). As Mary Beard (1990, p. 11) noted

> Libraries are not simply the storehouses of books. They are the means of organizing knowledge and . . . of controlling that knowledge and restricting access to it. They are symbols of intellectual and political power, and the far from innocent focus of conflict and opposition. It is hardly for reasons of simple security that so many of our great libraries are built on the model of fortresses.

All of us dedicated to the belief that our essential commitments should be to the unproblematic and transcendent values of books and reading might benefit from reflection on Lakota Sioux Russel Means's (1983, p. 19) cutting reminder:

> I detest writing. The process itself epitomizes the European concept of "legitimate" thinking; what is written has an importance that is denied the spoken . . . . It is one of the white world's ways of destroying the cultures of non-European peoples, the imposing of an abstraction over the spoken relationship of a people . . . . It seems that the only way to communicate with the white world is through the dead, dry leaves of a book.

In short, the old defense against a more proactive approach to library and information service has lost its persuasive power. It is time for the library profession to acknowledge the extent to which library and information service has been fully embedded in the political economy of the West, and to confront squarely the contradictions inherent in the idea of free library service in a post-industrial society. As one recent commentator put it, "hiding behind neutrality" no longer seems to be an option (Gremmels, 1991).

It is our hope that at the very least the contents of this chapter will disabuse librarians of the idea that library and information service represents an independent, apolitical, and neutral element in American society, and arm them with fact and theory that will prepare the way for a critical and collective meditation on the essential foundations of professional authority in library and information science.

5

Work in the Post-Industrial Era

Toto, I have the feeling we're not in Kansas anymore.

Dorothy in the Wizard of Oz

The nation's industrial past plays no part in our vision of the future.

Kathryn Marie Dudley

INTRODUCTION

It is now essential that we examine the implications of the emerging post-industrial society, or information age, for the workplace. Virtually all students of the
subject suggest that the nature of work, and work arrangements, will be dramatically impacted by what Daniel Bell has defined as "intellectual technology."
That is, the emergence of a "computer-assisted 'theoretical knowledge' univer-
salized by telecommunications" (Archer, 1990, p. 107) has the potential to revolutionize the nature of work in the post-industrial era. As H. V. Savitch (1988, p.
5) noted

> Boiled down, post-industrialism is a broad phenomenon that can be gauged along
> multiple dimensions. It encompasses change in *what* we do to earn a livelihood (pro-
> cessing or services rather than manufacturing) as well as *how* we do it (brains rather
> than hands) and *where* we do it (offices rather than factories).

103

Ironically, while Bell (1980a) argues that the post-industrial era may well have a "decisive" impact on "the character of the occupations and work in which men engage" (p. 501), he offers very little serious analysis of how he feels the technology will impact on the workplace. Numerous scholars have noted this blindspot in Bell's scenario, and have gone further to suggest that his brief remarks on the question are hopelessly utopian and too often contradictory. Margaret Archer (1990) notes that the result is an unconvincing and casual attempt to rewrite Emile Durkheim's (1984) classic *Division of Labor in Society* "with a happy ending" (p. 101). Thus, while Bell is not nearly as useful in analyzing the nature of the post-industrial workplace (as opposed to his amazingly accurate predictions about the nature of the emerging "intellectual technology"), we must nevertheless attend to his conclusions before turning in other directions for more fruitful analysis of this pivotal issue.

A careful student of Bell's work will find it full of provocative and often contradictory comments on the nature of work in the post-industrial era, but little can be found in the way of thorough projections. Perhaps the most forceful and suggestive remark Bell (1989, p. 171) has made on this fundamental question is the following:

> If character is defined by work, then we shall see a society where "nature" is largely excluded and "things" are largely excluded within the experience of persons. If more and more individuals are in work situations that involve a "game between persons", clearly more and more questions of equity and "comparable worth" will arise. The nature of hierarchy in work may be increasingly questioned, and new modes of participation may be called for. All of these portend huge changes in the structures of organization from those we have seen in older models.

The implication seems to be that the post-industrial era will mandate an end to the rigidly hierarchical organization structure so characteristic of contemporary life, and will rather naturally lead to the undermining of the longstanding and institutionalized exclusionary and discriminatory practices so commonly reflected in gender and racial labor market segmentation in 20th century America. Even more clear is the fact that the post-industrial era will dictate a change in "the places *where* people work" and "the *kind* of work they do" (Bell, 1973a, p. 134).

Judith Perrole (1991) has noted that Bell's adherents "argue that computers will enhance the quality and working conditions of intellectual labor, freeing humans *from* the drudgery of routine mental activity and freeing them *for* creative thought" (p. 222). They do not fear the computer, for they endorse Bell's belief in "growing egalitarianism" in the post-industrial workplace, and insist that "knowledge engineering applications should not reduce the wages, autonomy, or skill of employees in the professional, managerial, and higher level technical categories" (p. 223).

While many students of the post-industrial workplace have found Bell's suggestion that the information age will mandate new organizational structures of use in analyzing our future, others are troubled by his adamant opposition to affirmative action and quota programs designed to reduce *deliberately* the extent of racial and gender discrimination in the workplace. While all hope that his optimistic conclusion that the end of smokestack America and the emergence of the information and service economy will herald the creation of a safer, more rewarding, and more meritocratic working environment, many still fear that longstanding discriminatory and exploitive workplace relationships will remain in place unless deliberate and forceful action is taken to eliminate these practices. It should come as no surprise to find that women and people of color are less sanguine about the post-industrial workplace than are well educated white males.

While the contours of the changing post-industrial workplace are more clearly outlined today than they were in 1973, when Bell published *The Coming of Post-Industrial Society*, there nevertheless remains a great deal of controversy over the future of work in the information age. It is now time to turn to a systematic analysis of the literature on the nature of work in the future.

CONTRA-BELL: HARRY BRAVERMAN AND THE DEGRADATION AND DESKILLING OF WORK IN POST-INDUSTRIAL AMERICA

One year after the publication of Bell's *The Coming of Post-Industrial Society* sociologists of work encountered another book which was to stimulate a firestorm of debate and a tidal wave of research. Harry Braverman's *Labor and Monopoly Capital: The Degradation of Work in the Twentieth Century* (1974) appeared at the very moment when workers and sociologists of work alike were awakening to the problems and potential of the post-industrial workplace. The stage was set for a major confrontation between Braverman and Bell, for Braverman's work directly contradicted Bell's scenario in almost every particular. That is, where Bell forecast a significant reorganization of the workplace in the new "game between persons," Braverman saw only further centralization and management authoritarianism. Where Bell projected a workforce that would be considerably "upskilled," Braverman insisted that the workers would be further "deskilled." Where Bell glimpsed only more rewarding and fulfilling work, Braverman noticed intensifying worker alienation and the steady "degradation" of work. What became all too clear to serious students of the sociology of work in American society was that one of them had it wrong. But which one?

The search for the one true prophet is the subject of most of this chapter. But at the outset we might note that the empirical work stimulated by the obvious contradictions in the theories put forward by Bell and Braverman has grown into a significant corpus of scholarship which is increasingly hard to concisely categorize (for a variety of maps see Kai Erikson & Steven Vallas, 1990). One should not be surprised to learn in advance that the results of empirical work designed to test the theses put forward by Bell and Braverman have tended to run at some highly eccentric angles (Grint, 1991).

In trying to sort out this huge and rapidly growing body of research we might best begin with the observation that Braverman's ideas initially met with a surprisingly positive reception given their dark and foreboding predictions about work in post-industrial America. Within a decade the "Braverman thesis" had generated a large body of research along a wide ranging front all gathered, by students of the subject, under the rubric of "the labor process school" of the sociology of work. Braverman had insisted that what was most striking about the post-industrial workplace was its similarities and continuities with the industrial workplace. Building on Marxist scholarship, he reminded his readers that the essential dynamic of the capitalist system was the profit motive. He carefully documented the extent to which capitalists tended to maximize profits by exploiting workers. Braverman suggested that this was most commonly done by "Taylorizing" work. By this he meant that employers were always tempted to simplify work tasks, utilizing a variety of systems analysis techniques, and once this process was complete management would rob the workers of their skills and replace skilled workers with a more pliant and less expensive workforce. Braverman viewed the emergence of information technology as "an integral part of the struggle between labor and capital" which lead to "proletarianizing" of the workforce (Webster & Robins, 1986, p. 129).

The outcome, virtually inevitable, was that workers would be steadily and consistently deskilled and the quality of work in American society would be continuously degraded. Braverman (1974, p. 119) put it this way:

> Thus, if the first principle is the gathering and the development of knowledge of labor processes, and the second is the concentration of this knowledge as the exclusive province of management—together with its essential converse, the absence of such knowledge among the workers—then the third is the *use of this monopoly over knowledge to control each step of the labor process and its mode of execution.*

He implied that professionals were not immune to this deskilling and degrading of their work, and he suggested that it was only a matter of time before professionals would encounter the fate of craft workers in the capitalist workplace.

Immediately upon publication of Braverman's work a large number of scholars, skeptical of Bell's upbeat scenario for the post-industrial workforce, set out to test the "Braverman thesis" in every corner of the post-industrial workplace. Judith Perrole (1991, p. 225) summarized the research agenda in this way:

> If information itself is seen as a commodity produced for profit by the rational organization and mechanization of intellectual labor, then information can be produced by the computer in the same way that products were made by the factory machinery

of the first industrial revolution—through the alienation of laborers from the production process.

Early studies seemed to confirm much of the Braverman thesis. For instance, Philip Kraft (1979, p. 17) studied the impact of IT on computer programming and concluded that

> It is clear . . . that programming has experienced a steady process of fragmentation and routinization while programmers as a group have experienced a rapid deskilling. These trends call into question the major claim of technology advocates, that increasingly sophisticated technology in the workplace creates jobs that are better than those it displaces.

And historian David Nobel (1977, 1984) has examined the development of industrial automation and discovered a story that supports Braverman's thesis in many particulars.

Particularly forceful support for the Braverman thesis was found in Barbara Garson's (1988) study of office work entitled *The Electronic Sweatshop: How Computers Are Transforming the Office of the Future into the Factory of the Past*. In that work Garson (p. 263) concluded that

> Any system that expends so much money and energy on limiting instead of using human creativity has got to be inefficient. Yet the individuals now making the basic decisions about white-collar automation assume that the best way to run things is to further centralize control—with themselves in command.

It must be noted that the picture has become less clear with time. As more and more studies have accumulated testing the Bell and Braverman theories, we have been able to develop a more detailed and complex picture of the emerging post-industrial workplace which confirms (and undermines) aspects of both theories. Paul Attewell (1987) summarizes the evidence as follows by pointing out that Braverman's "notion that deskilling is the dominant tendency across the whole economy" is not borne out by the evidence (p. 325). He notes that, while "few scholars believe that deskilling never occurs," it is apparent that deskilling is not the "secular trend" identified by Braverman, and that it has not been the fate of the working class in the post-industrial era (p. 341). William Form (1987) agrees and notes that while deskilling does, indeed, occur, it does not seem to be the dominant theme in the post-industrial workplace.

A study of trends in Europe drew similar conclusions. Martin Baethge and Herbert Oberbeck (1989, p. 120) summarized their findings in the following way:

> In contrast to a widespread viewpoint, we do not believe that the introduction of modern technology in the administrative sector will lead to a new phase of Taylorism in work that is principally intellectual in nature. The hypothesis that the work

carried out by white-collar workers will also be characterized by increased division of labor, parceling of work, loss of content, loss of qualifications, and monotony, and that, at best, only a small, elite group of controllers sitting in management would not be affected . . . does not stand up to an empirical test.

The Committee on New American Realities of the National Planning Association (Doeringer et al. 1991, p. 105) provides a careful summary of the data and nicely illustrates the extent to which the two theories need to be transcended in the search for the future of the post-industrial workplace. Their conclusions deserve extensive quotation:

> Aggregate studies suggest that technological change has been largely neutral with respect to skills mix. Technological change has resulted in neither significant upgrading nor significant downgrading in overall skills requirements.

However, they also point out that

> This benign view of technological change results from aggregate data that mask off-setting positive and negative disruptions in the labor market caused by such change . . . . It can also result in skill obsolescence, worker displacement, and unemployment. Individual firms, industries, and regions can therefore suffer significant, often irreparable, losses from technological change.

The conviction that information technology will deskill and degrade labor (the Braverman thesis) still remains very widespread both in the United States and abroad. A number of powerful and angry books have appeared in recent years which extend or deepen Braverman's ideas and draw dire conclusions about the future of work in America. One of the most influential of these is the work of Stanley Aronowitz and William DiFazio entitled *The Jobless Future* (1994). "The tendency of science to dominate the labor process," they argue, "now heralds an entirely new regime of work in which almost no production skills are required." They explain (p. 20) this conclusion in the following way:

> Older forms of technical or professional knowledge are transformed, incorporated, superseded, or otherwise eliminated by computer-mediated technologies . . . . But, unlike the mechanizing era of pulleys and electrically powered machinery . . . computers have transferred most knowledge associated with the crafts and manual labor, and, increasingly, intellectual knowledge, to the machine. As a result, while each generation of technological change makes some work more complex and interesting and raises the level of training or qualification required . . . for the overwhelming majority of workers, this process simplifies tasks or eliminates them, and thus eliminates the worker.

This dark vision of a world headed unerringly toward massive unemployment is seconded by another troubling new work by Jeremy Rifkin entitled The *End of*

Work (1995). Insisting that "the Information Age has arrived," Rifkin goes on to note (p. xv):

> In the years ahead, new, more sophisticated software technologies are going to bring civilization ever closer to a near-workerless world . . . . The wholesale substitution of machines for workers is going to force every nation to rethink the role of human beings in the social process.

While it is hard to read the empirical work on the subject as suggesting anything so dramatic, it does appear that the huge investment in information technology in the United States is beginning to reap substantial benefits. Initially, these investments were clearly "wasted" in the sense that they produced no visible gains in productivity (Landauer, 1995). However, in about 1993 this productivity gap narrowed and then dissapeared (Fallows, 1996). What now seems clear is that more and more information commodities are now being produced with fewer and fewer workers (Burstein & Kline, 1995), and indeed, with little visible improvement in the educational attainments of the workforce at large (Head, 1996). The impact of these improvements in productivity has been devastating for industrial workforces in the United States and elsewhere. Kathryn Marie Dudley (1994, p. 177) highlighted the nature of the change with this eloquent meditation:

> In the ritual symbolism of postindustrial society, industrial workers have become the new American primitive. They are people who work with their hands in a society that increasingly values work done with the mind. Their social distance from the new cultural ideal is measured and legitimated by educational credentials. If they wish to survive in the modern age and claim a place in the middle class, it is said, they will have to educate themselves to do the kind of work demanded of people living in a postindustrial society . . . . the nation's industrial past plays no part in our vision of the future.

The situation has progressed to the point in the United States that we find the champions of industrial labor counseling a "neo-Luddite" resistance to information technology similar to the futile struggle of the Luddites in their war against the Industrial Revolution nearly two hundred years ago (Sale, 1995). Others, less concerned, point calmly to the fact that the U.S. economy remains healthy and, most notably, that the unemployment rate in early 1997 hovered around a remarkably low 5 percent.

Thus, we find that the research is as contradictory in 1998 as it was in 1974. As Magali Larson (1980) noted early in the debate, "we may now be facing either the proletarianization of new social categories . . . or the ascension of a new class [of information professionals] or both things" (p. 171). Judith Perrole (1991, p. 231) noticed the same ambiguity in the current workplace environment when she wrote

In both an economic and cultural sense, and regardless of the outcome of the deskilling debate, the spread of knowledge engineering will devalue some kinds of mental labor. In the economic sense, professional, technical and managerial employees who do the kind of thinking that machines do (or that inexpensive labor does with machines) will see a relative reduction in their wages and salaries unless they can acquire new tasks to protect their existing areas of expertise from automation.

PERSISTENT LABOR MARKET SEGMENTATION IN THE POST-INDUSTRIAL WORKPLACE

One of the most consistent supports for the Braverman thesis, and one of the most troubling aspects of the emerging post-industrial workplace, is the overwhelming evidence that the post-industrial workplace promises to be as discriminatory and exclusionary as the industrial workplace. Recall Daniel Bell's rosy prediction that the post-industrial era would mandate a dramatic restructuring of the workplace along more affirmative and participatory lines, and contrast that with the evidence and one is forced to the unavoidable conclusion that Bell's predictions were too optimistic.

A trend in the research on the information workforce that should be particularly troubling to members of the library profession is the consistent evidence that women are faring considerably less well than their male counterparts. Study after study confirms this trend. For instance, Pamela Kramer and Sheila Lehman (1990, p. 5) reviewed the evidence and found that "female computer professionals are disproportionately concentrated in lower paid and less prestigious jobs," and this finding is confirmed by Perry and Greber (1990). In a thorough review of the evidence Ginzberg, Noyelle, and Stanback (1986, p. 27) concluded

A large share of the rapidly increasing service sector employment has involved work traditionally done by women at low pay. Throughout the period there was a marked tendency for much of the new white-collar work to be defined as women's work, paid for at relatively low rates, and performed by women.

Cynthia Cockburn (1988) directly confronted Bell's rosy scenario when she noted that "a sexual division of labour in and around technology persists" and that women have made little progress in the high status fields that Bell defines as "intellectual technology." She concludes that (pp. 11–12)

The consistent theme unfolding here is this: women are to be found in great numbers *operating* machinery, and some operating jobs are more skill-demanding than others. But women continue to be rarities in those occupations that involve knowing about what goes on inside the machine. The electronic revolution is making little difference. The flexible, transferable skills of engineering are still the property of males. With few exceptions, the designer and developer of the new systems, the people who market and sell, install, manage and service machinery, are men.

This should not come as a surprise, for despite what Daniel Bell may have suggested, Cockburn insists that "it was a false hope to suppose that the short leap from the electro-mechanical to the electronic stage of technology could do for women what two revolutions in the entire mode of production had failed to accomplish" (p. 226).

While the trends appear relatively clear to this point at least, there is less agreement on the reasons for the persistence of labor market segmentation (Hughes, 1996). Part of the explanation is clearly blatant discrimination, for as Barbara Reskin (1988) notes men have great "incentive to preserve their advantages" and possess the "ability to do so by establishing the rules that distribute rewards" (p. 58). Women, like Reskin and Jerry Jacobs (1989), insist that the idea that such job segregation will simply (and quite naturally) disappear is unrealistic and they, and likeminded women, call for vigorous political and legal action to halt the unending discrimination against women.

Others argue that the information technology itself is gendered. Jan Zimmerman (1983) concluded that what we are witnessing is the "encoding of old values on new technologies." Lana Rakow (1988) argues that "technology is based on the dominant masculine value system of Western culture," and concludes that "technologies are used to construct and maintain gender differences and hierarchies" (pp. 57, 67, see also Jansen, 1989; Morgall, 1993). In a thorough review of the research on the subject Judy Wajcman (1991) concludes that male power is literally "embodied in the design of technology" and that "the workplace culture based on technical skill, which expresses and consolidates relations among men, is an important factor in explaining the continuing exclusion of women from skilled work" (pp. 29–30).

Other studies demonstrate the extent to which women lack the technical training necessary to take advantage of the emerging opportunities in the post-industrial era. These studies suggest that unless this situation is attacked "the girls of today will have no choice but to be second-class citizens in the computer-intensive world of tomorrow" (Kiesler, Sproull, & Eccles, 1985, p. 452). Jerry Jacobs (1989), however, suggests that education alone probably does not hold the solution, for "there is a great deal of occupation segregation by sex among men and women with similar levels of educational attainment" (p. 192). She concludes that under current circumstances progress for a few elite women will only mask the continued discrimination against the majority of working women.

Study after study of the occupations that might be considered potential members of the new high status information professions bear out these unsettling conclusions. For instance, Perry and Greber (1990) concluded that "women's increasing representation among computer personnel thus parallels their experience in most fields: ghettoization in low status, low pay, 'deskilled' job categories" (p. 87). Linda Christian-Smith (1991) examined women in book publishing and found that "while this new technology has de-skilled work in publishing in general, this has been especially the case in the editorial departments, which are predominantly female" (p. 51).

Librarianship does not appear to be immune to these continuing trends. James Grimm (1988) notes that even fields like librarianship, where 85 percent of the professionals are women, afford fewer rewards for the female members of the profession "even when experience and qualifications are similar" (p. 308). Sociologist and library educator Leigh Estabrook (1984) concluded that the information era promised little to library women for "from the evidence available, it would seem that women's opportunities in this changing field are not going to be significantly altered" (p. 170). As recently as 1995, J. Michael Pemberton and Christine R. Nugent (p. 126) concluded that

> Continued use of such terms as "the information society," "the information economy," "knowledge worker," and the "information explosion" suggests that information is an increasingly important social, political, and economic resource. Curiously, however, those occupational fields traditionally associated with the selection, acquisition, organization, maintenance, and dissemination of information . . . have not seen the development in size, visability, and stature that one would expect in an emergent "information society."

Other women see the problem as much more complicated than a simple gender discrimination model would suggest. Beverly Burris (1989) argues that the post-industrial era promises to "structure economic opportunity in new and yet gendered ways" and that what we are witnessing is a "more complex fabric of gender discrimination." She presents a case for a more subtle awareness of the ways in which the "bifurcation into expert and nonexpert sectors, a process that is correlated with gender, race and class segregation" suggests that the future promises an environment where "different groups of women face different types of discrimination and fundamentally different workplace opportunities" (p. 166).

Two authors who have carefully examined the opportunities of women in the post-industrial era, with its emphasis on computers and intellectual technology, are Bernice Carroll and Lorraine Code. Carroll (1990) argues that women are particularly vulnerable in a post-industrial environment which is dominated by theoretical and technical developments in "intellectual technology." She documents the way that men have always defined women's ideas as "unoriginal" thus legitimating the exclusion of women from the "upper ranks of the class system of the intellect." She sees no diminution in this "phallocratic" tendency and concludes that it promises to perpetuate the segmented labor market (p. 136):

> The concept of "originality," though essentially empty of substantive meaning, is used today to justify and rationalize a class system based upon claims of property in ideas. This system assigns most men and almost all women to positions in the lower

classes and preserves for a small group of self-recruiting males both hegemony over received knowledge and control of a variety of rewards and privileges.

Lorraine Code (1991) agrees and critically analyzes the long standing male practice of devaluing the intellectual capabilities of women. Beginning with Aristotle's insistence that "the slave has no deliberative faculty at all; the woman has, *but it is without authority,* and the child has, but it is immature," Code goes on to demonstrate the extent to which "latter-day variants of Aristotle's contentions about women's lack of rational authority shape women's professional lives and areas of earned expertise" (pp. 181, 223). Insisting that these "convictions seem to ensure that women's cognitive authority will remain as limited as it has been throughout the history of modern knowledge," Code counsels "continuous refusal" if women are ever to "claim the power to assume authoritative, expert status on their terms" in the post-industrial era (pp. 232, 219).

Thus, while it is apparent that Braverman's dark and foreboding predictions about the deskilling of the post-industrial workplace are not fully supported by the evidence, it is also clear that female members of the workforce face continued discrimination, especially in the high status information professions (Hughes, 1996). This fact presents special problems for a "female-intensive" field, like library and information science, and has the potential to thwart the aspirations of individual librarians and the profession alike. Christine L. Williams (1995) notes that it's "Still a Man's World," especially in feminized fields like nursing, social work and librarianship. She insists (p. 45) that women face a sort of double jeopardy in feminized fields like librarianship, for on the one hand, library women lack political power which might enable them to enhance their professional status:

> This lack of power is linked to the general devaluation of women, and the work they do, in society. Indeed, sociologists have found it to be the case that cross-culturally, the work women do is of "lesser status"—regardless of the actual nature of the work.

On the other hand, library women find that they are being surpassed by the small minority of men that choose librarianship as a career. Williams refers to this dilemma as the "glass escalator effect" and uses this model to explain why library women so consistently appear to be less "successful" than their male counterparts in librarianship.

Roma Harris (1993, p. 874) has addressed the oddly ignored idea of librarianship as a feminized field in the digital era by demanding that we acknowledge "the fact that, for more than 100 years, library work in North America has been woman's work" if we ever hope to "grasp what is going on in librarianship today." Insisting that the "service ideal" so characteristic of the nurturing work done by women in American librarianship is being undermined by the twin currents of the pursuit of male-stream professionalism and the indiscriminate deployment of information technology.

The pursuit of a male-stream model of professionalism, Harris contends, will destroy our commitment to our clients' best interests and force us into an unworkable embrace of information-as-commodity and a "pay-per" mentality that is incompatible with the "female traditions of library work." She also argues that the deployment of information technology threatens to systematically deskill the field, robbing librarians of their expert knowledge of cataloging (following Braverman) and further undervaluing their work. Noting that there are dangers involved for librarianship if the idea of professional status is pursued too intensely, Harris warns that the "twin beliefs that technology is the key to a higher-status future and that professionalism can be achieved by avoiding undervalued (i.e., female) work—may well result in the complete erosion of the profession of librarianship" (1993, p. 876).

While her work is powerful and passionate (R. Harris, 1992, 1993, 1995-96), her suggestion that librarians should strengthen their commitment to selfless service to patrons, and that "librarians who wish to stop the erosion of their profession must stop shunning the female traditions of library work" (1993, p. 876), presents a real problem for the library profession. Her insistence that librarians acknowledge their "woman-centered history" seems to come coupled with an insistence that librarians remain rigidly opposed to change. She would even seem to be suggesting that any widespread commitment to the "information paradigm" among librarians will destroy the profession and handicap our most needy information users. That is, attempts to move into the information "business" are both foolhardy and treasonous.

Roma Harris is not alone in counseling resistance to the imperitives of the information era. Walt Crawford and Michael Gorman (1995) have written an equally conservative tract that has proven extremely popular among librarians. After acknowledging the feminized nature of the field, they insist that librarians remain true to "the realities of libraries" which Gorman defines as the truth that "the library has stood like a rock in the swift current of history—unchanging." (p. vii). Insisting that the cultural mission of the library is under attack by "barbarians" and "technovandals" Crawford and Gorman, like Roma Harris, counsel extreme caution as the profession moves into the information era.

Despite this underside of the post-industrial era it is still important to emphasize and examine the ways in which the nature of the workplace appears to be changing. As we examine the latest research on this subject, we will find some support for Bell's "happy ending" and even, perhaps, some evidence to support the claim that the new workplace will reflect a more gender neutral attitude in the future.

SHOSHANA ZUBOFF ON THE INFORMATED WORKPLACE OF THE INFORMATION ERA

In 1978, Harvard Business School Professor Shosana Zuboff set out to attempt to resolve the contradictions inherent in the theories of Daniel Bell and Harry

Braverman. Convinced that the American workplace was on the "edge of a historical transformation of immense proportions" as the result of the emergence of "information technology" in the workplace, Zuboff (1988, p. xiii) wanted to understand the way in which worker's lives would be transformed in the post-industrial era,

> assumptions about knowledge and power, their beliefs about work and the meaning they derived from it, the content and rhythm of their social exchanges, and the ordinary mental and physical disciplines to which they accommodated in their daily lives.

She was troubled by the extent to which Bell's views on these questions were limited to "sociological abstractions," and she launched an ambitious series of empirical studies of the changing American workplace in order to (p. xiv)

> Understand the practical problems that would have to be confronted in order to manage the new computerized workplace in ways that would fulfill the lofty promise of a knowledge-based society and to generate knowledge that would be instructive to those charged with that managerial responsibility.

The result, after 10 years of work, was the publication of her extremely influential book entitled *In the Age of the Smart Machine: The Future of Work and Power* (1988).

In that work Zuboff concludes that information technology promises to transform the American workplace fundamentally. She readily admits that Braverman's insistence that the dynamic of organizational management tempts managers to extend their "exclusive control of the organization's knowledge base" is clearly in evidence, but that the "informated" workplace promises to undermine such rigid and hierarchical control as it becomes increasingly clear to managers that the old emphasis on certainty and control is becoming decidedly *unproductive*. That is, while she acknowledges the validity of Braverman's insistence that managers attempt to generate profit by exploiting labor, she also insists that Daniel Bell is correct in arguing that the new "computer-mediated" workplace demands a new approach to organizational structure.

Based on her careful empirical work she concludes that while management may well resist change in the organization and control of the production process, the post-industrial era mandates "innovative methods of information sharing and social exchange" that will eventually lead to "a deepened sense of collective responsibility and joint ownership, as access to ever-broader domains of information lend new objectivity to data and preempt the dictates of hierarchical authority" (p. 7). She argues that the informated organizations of the post-industrial era will transcend the "stale reproduction of the past" and will, instead, take advantage of this "historic opportunity to more fully develop the economic and human potential of our work organizations" (p. 7).

The key insight in Zuboff's work seems to be the notion that while *the bottom line* will continue to control organizational structure and management style that same attention to the profit motive will mandate the more affirmative and participatory workplace organization hinted at by Daniel Bell. In short, the old hierarchical and rigidly centralized management structures that so characterized American capitalism in the industrial era will prove *inefficient* in the post-industrial era, and the profit motive will drive managers to adopt more participatory styles.

Thus, we can now see the outlines of an emerging consensus. While Braverman's thesis explains the industrial workplace, it is Daniel Bell who appears to have glimpsed the changes mandated by the post-industrial era. Other scholars agree with Zuboff when she insists that the very dynamic of a capitalist system will mandate this change as managers seek to increase productivity and profit margins. While we are clearly in a transitional stage where both management styles are in evidence, it seems clear that computer-mediated work in the informated workplace will require a "major restructuring of work-roles" (Strassmann, 1985, p. 245). Larry Hirschhorn (1984) saw the same trend when he demonstrated that "postindustrial skill" will demand that workers be constantly involved in "the process of active learning, direct intervention in the machine system, and progressive widening of their knowledge" (p. 163). Lee Sproull and Sara Kiesler (1991, p. 175), after an intense study of the networked workplace, concluded that while we are clearly in a transitional phase, the wave of the future appears to mandate

> a flexible, internally motivated, continuously learning work force; a strong internal culture to support information sharing and participation in problem solving; delegation or shared responsibility in recognition that dispersed activity requires local action and flexibility . . . and creation of dynamic procedures, structures, and groupings to amplify expertise and technology.

IT: CHALLENGE FOR THE NEXT DECADE

John Sculley (1991, p. 56) effectively articulates a fundamental aspect of organizational life when he notes that

> There is a dangerous timelag built into even the most successful institutions. They are created at one time in response to some particular opportunity in a given historical context. And then as the context shifts, the institution finds itself carrying excess baggage that is no longer useful.

F. W. Lancaster (1991a) is clearly correct when he concludes that "on the whole, the [library] profession has been neither imaginative nor innovative in its exploitation of technology" (p. 4). Unlike Seiler and Surprenant (1991), who remain confident that the "technological solutions to the problems surrounding libraries are forthcoming" (p. 29), Lancaster (1991a, pp. 12–13) has become more pessimistic in his assessment of information technology's impact on libraries:

> But let us not delude ourselves into believing that it [information technology] has had a substantial impact in improving the services that a library provides to its users, that it has greatly improved the image of the librarian, or that technology alone will increase the perceived value of library and librarian in the future.

The failure to exploit information technology has certainly not been limited to libraries. All organizations, including those in the for-profit sector, have struggled with the promise and problems inherent in information technology. Keen (1991) claims that during the past three decades the "effective use of rapidly changing technology has lagged behind its availability" (p. 212). Part of the problem, of course, is that the rate of change in many organizations has occurred so rapidly that management has not had time to adapt to it (Keen, 1991, p. 210). A more fundamental problem is that the difficulty of integrating information technology into an organization has been seriously underestimated. Libraries, like many other organizations, have been slow to recognize that implementing information technology requires more than buying a computer and software from a vendor (Matthews, 1980, p. 114). The reliance of most libraries on "turnkey" systems has also fostered the erroneous view that implementing information systems is as simple as flipping a switch. Unfortunately, as Epstein (1991) notes, "although one might be led to believe (or hope or dream) that buying a turnkey automated library system means that implementation is as simple as turning the key in a new automobile, this is not the case" (p. 168).

Libraries are complex systems in which the technical, organizational, and social components are mutually interdependent. A change in any part of the system will have an immediate impact on the rest of the system. While the exact shape of the changes that information technology will have on libraries and library operations cannot be predicted, there is overwhelming evidence indicating that (1) change will be the norm of the future, (2) information technology will continue its rapid development for at least the next decade, and (3) information technology will become increasingly critical to the success or failure of libraries. There is one last prediction that can be safely made: the integration of information technology into libraries will not be done easily, quickly, or cheaply. This fact, too often overlooked by the paperless society cheerleaders, grows out of a complex set of variables, such as the historical tradition that so strongly controls the discussion of the library in contemporary society, the lack of sophisticated understanding of information technology and its uses, inadequate attention to the implementation problems inherent in the utilization of information technology, and resistance to change in management styles among American library leaders.

Thus, once again we must conclude that the picture is not nearly as clear as some would have us believe. Information technology does, indeed, appear to be a fundemental reality in the future of library and information services in the United States and many other nations throughout the world. However, we have little foundation for claiming that we know much about the direction or extent of the impact of information technology in libraries. We have only begun to glimpse the promise and the pitfalls, and it remains to be seen whether the library profession can bring the technology, a clear sense of mission, and the competent personnel together in a successful attempt to bring library and information service into the post-industrial era.

Despite the need for caution, it does appear clear that organizational structures and management styles will have to change (Boyett & Conn, 1992). Hierarchical and centralized management structures will be steadily undermined by the constant demand for speed and flexibility. Shoshana Zuboff's (1988) claim that organizations will, by necessity, become more participatory and open seems supported by research in both the sociology of work and information technology. And, Hirschorn's (1984) insistence that such change will offer more rewarding and challenging opportunities for information professionals is also persuasive. With enhanced opportunity will also come new responsibilities. Library and information professionals will find that they must be constantly involved in both "the learning organization" and the decision making process. Information technology is no panacea. But properly deployed, it offers the potential to enhance both the professional opportunities of librarians and the quality of service offered to the clients who depend upon their services.

6

Conclusion:
A Prologue to Library and
Information Services in the
Post-Industrial Era

In reality, there is not one moment that does not bring with it its own revolutionary possibility—it only wants to be defined as a specific one, namely as the chance for a totally new resolution in view of a totally new task.

Walter Benjamin

All fixed, fast-frozen relations, with their train of ancient and venerable prejudices and opinions, are swept away . . . All that is solid melts into air.

Karl Marx

There is nothing more difficult to carry out, nor more doubtful of success, nor more dangerous to handle, than to intiate a new order of things.

Machiavelli

"ALL THAT IS SOLID MELTS INTO AIR"

In the August 15, 1991 issue of the *New York Review of Books*, Patrice Higonnet wrote an essay that nicely encapsulated all of the dilemmas faced by librarians as they enter the post-industrial era. Entitled "Scandal on the Seine," Higonnet's work reflects on the controversy surrounding the choice of the architectural design for the new Bibliotheque de France (Bloch & Hesse, 1995), and concludes that the design constitutes "a librarian's nightmare" (p. 32). Given that conclusion, Higonnet (p. 33) tries to understand the reasons behind the selection of a design which seems to deemphasize the fact that the French National Library is a *library*! He notes

> It seems . . . plausible to suppose the architects and managers of this devastating project simply think that books are on their way out. They may well believe that what once would have been in print will soon be electronified, microfilmed, and microfiched. In this view there will never be many books in the towers, and if there are and if they do decompose, it won't really matter because all those pages will be on CD-ROM, on-line periodicals, and computer screens.

Higonnet then clearly states the problem of library planners faced at once with "the overwhelming counterweight of historical tradition" and the pressure to confront the future (p. 33):

> The French are at once the most modern-minded and the most tradition-bound of European nations. They cherish an aristocratic past, but they are fascinated by computer processing—"*l'informatique*"—and the aura surrounding sleek modern technology.

Higonnet readily acknowledges the need for "a computerized catalog system as well as the full range of modern techniques for reproducing and storing information," but insists that the new design for the Bibliotheque de France represents an irresponsible "gamble on the survival of an irreplaceable collection that carries their nation's collective memory" (p. 33).

It is apparent that this controversy represents the dilemma of all of us who are trying to think seriously about the future of library and information service in the post-industrial era. For while we readily acknowledge the promise of the new intellectual technology for the improvement of information services in the post-industrial era, we are also increasingly aware of the real dangers to libraries which have always acted as "their nation's collective memory." Our responsibility as professional librarians is to discover a way to steer responsibly a course between the Scylla of an uncritical embrace of an as yet non-existent future and the Charybdis of a reactionary commitment to a barely workable past.

We began this book by noting that we, like Hanna Arendt (1951), were writing "against a background of both reckless optimism and reckless despair" (p. vii).

This condition has been prompted, as Michael Gorman (1991) points out, by the "perception that the increase in the influence of electronic technology could or will cause a fundamental change in the structures of scholarship and librarianship" (pp. 74–75). Gorman gets right to the point (p. 75) when he reflects that

> An existential terror has seized some librarians, causing them to doubt the future of librariarnship and even of libraries themselves. This *angst* leads them to seek refuge in the vacuities of "information science" and even to declare themselves no longer librarians but "information professionals."

He goes on to note that the peculiar form of "professional suicide" is misdirected if it is designed to impress the scholarly community whose "world is fueled, in small part, by the flow of 'information,' but no scholar can live on information alone and will regard its purveyor as, at best, a useful supplier of a relatively unimportant service" (p. 75).

As stated in the preface, we set out to provide the foundation for a more responsible and enlightened discussion of the implications of the information age for library and information services, a new awareness that might help us to avoid our special "existential terror" and overcome the rhetoric of "reckless optimism and reckless despair." We have now completed that task, at least as best as *we* can, and yet we are reluctant to leave this project without presenting our own hesitant suggestions relative to the important task facing library and information professionals as we enter the 21st century.

TOTALITY AND VISION: LIBRARY AND INFORMATION SERVICE ON THE POST-INDUSTRIAL "LANDSCAPE"

Sharon Zukin (1991) notes that the idea of "landscape" has come to mean considerably more than just "physical surroundings" or a genre in art, but has taken on the much more sophisticated sense of "an ensemble of material and social practices and their symbolic representation" (p. 16). As such, the idea of the landscape of the post-industrial era nicely reflects our desire to engage our readers in a holistic exploration of the future of library and information services in the *context* of the emerging post-industrial era. While it remains for the reader to judge our success in meeting this objective, it needs to be emphasized that we feel one of the essential tasks facing librarians and information professionals is the need to break out of our narrow focus on "the library" and address the much more complex and extremely significant issue of the way in which library and information service is embedded in the post-industrial landscape.

As a result, following Zukin, our book's agenda has been shaped by the conviction that we must address a number of broad conceptual problems prior to the development of any useful understanding of the implications of the post-industrial era for library and information service. These concerns all revolve around the need to focus on the historical, economic, political, and *cultural* forces that are influencing the restructuring of library and information services in the post-indus-trial era, and forcing ourselves to confront the complex political economy, or landscape, of the information age in all of its interrelationships. This broader, even totalizing vision, is vital to understanding, and eventually directing, the future of library and information services in these changing times. In the pages that follow, we want to sketch briefly the ways in which these broad contextual issues might be "read" in order to provide us with at least tentative guidelines to our possible futures.

CAPITALISM, CAPITALISM, CAPITALISM

Some two centuries ago William Blackstone (1979) pointed to the fundamental underpinning of the capitalist economic system when he wrote (vol. 1, pp. 134–135)

> The third absolute right, [after life and liberty] inherent in every Englishman, is that of property: which consists in the free use, enjoyment, and disposal of all his acqui-sitions, without any control or diminution, save only by the laws of the land . . . . So great moreover is the regard of the law for private property that it will not authorize the least violation of it; no, not even for the general good of the whole community (book 1, par. 138).

Given this longstanding emphasis on private property as the cornerstone of capi-talism, and the evidence that information as a form of property was guaranteed in the Constitution, it comes as somewhat of a surprise to find librarians and liberals generally demonstrating so much concern over the "scandalous" extension of the commodity form to information.

As noted in Chapter 1, the paradox is explained by the fact that librarians have always viewed information—especially "political" information—as a "public good," and have generally insisted that "in a democracy, knowledge and informa-tion must in general be freely accessible" (Poster, 1990, p. 27). In this way the library liberals have defined information as a public good exempt from the rules governing the ownership and sale of private property. Framed in this political context information was viewed as essentially free of market constraints (Horow-itz, 1991). Librarians were encouraged to ignore the intensifying insistence that information was *the* commodity in the American economy, and overlook the evi-dence suggesting that the definition of information as a public good was proving less and less persuasive to more and more people. This is the significance of Mark Poster's (1990) remark that Bell "lends legitimacy to the extension of the com-modity form to the new realm of information" (p. 27). Librarians appear incapable of acknowledging the extent to which the idea of information as a public good in American society has been discredited or completely abandoned, and the degree to which the idea that information is the key commodity in the post-industrial marketplace has been adopted.

This tendency has led librarians to ignore the changing nature of the information marketplace, and stimulated them to take decidedly reactionary and uncritical official positions on the implications of the new "marketplace for ideas" in the post-industrial era. It is as if discussion of the role of the library in the 21st century could be legitimately carried out in terms that appeared sufficient in the 18th and 19th centuries, and as if librarians need only rehearse the founding myths in order to survive. In doing so we overlook the profound intuition articulated by Joseph Schumpeter (1950) some 50 years ago when he noted that "Capitalism, then, is by nature a form or method of economic change and not only never is but never can be stationary" (p. 82). Many have noted the intense energy of capitalism as its vital internal dynamic, but Schumpeter (p. 83) went on to argue for a simple truth when he insisted that this dynamic

> incessantly revolutionizes the economic structure *from within*, incessantly destroy-
> ing the old one, incessantly creating a new one. This process of Creative Destruction
> is the essential fact about capitalism.

Thus, Schumpeter points out, "the fundamental impulse that sets and keeps the capitalist engine in motion comes from the new consumers' goods, the new methods of production or transportation, the new markets, the new forms of industrial organization that capitalist enterprise creates" (p. 83). The emergence of a new commodity form—information—and new means of producing and marketing that new commodity form, and the displacement and elimination of old commodity forms, is, thus, best seen as part of the "perennial gale" of Creative Destruction at the very heart of the capitalist system. This is not to say that we must welcome the effects of such a dynamic, nor that we should not align ourselves in critical opposition to the implications of the idea of "information as a commodity," but it does suggest that we must abandon the disingenuous notion that nothing has changed, and abandon our increasingly fruitless commitment to blind resistance. The emergence of information as a central commodity form in the post-industrial era has initiated a wide ranging series of changes in the way in which the state, the capitalist system, and the people, view the *purpose* of information in the United States. It is this revolution in the purpose of information that, as Mark Poster (1990) points out, has made information "a privileged term in our culture" (p. 7). Thus, we are faced with what might be considered a paradigm shift, in the sense of Thomas Kuhn (1970), and while many of the trend lines are running at highly eccentric angles, it is increasingly clear that the "information paradigm" is (despite the anomalies) gaining strength within and without the library profession.

"Value orientations are," Judith Merkle (1980) points out, "an integral part of all sequential human activity designed to attain goals" (p. 278). Today we are faced with a changed landscape of values that defines information as the strategic economic resource in a new market culture that is "tied to the exchange-driven production, distribution, consumption, interpretation and reproduction of information" (Luke, 1989, p. 11). Linked to the increasing importance of information as a commodity is the rise of a host of developments designed to guarantee proprietary control of the information commodity. That is, one of the keys to the rise of information as *the* commodity form is the empowerment of capitalists who *own* information. This proprietary focus explains the intensifying tendency to define information as a private good that can be owned and sold on markets like other forms of private property.

This certain tendency in the new "marketplace of ideas" is of profound significance. For economists have known for years that the costs of creating information in a society that defines information primarily as a public good are prohibitively high for individual entrepreneurs. As Kenneth Arrow (quoted in Mowery & Rosenberg, 1989, pp. 5-6) put it in the context of research and development,

> Thus basic research, the output of which is only used as an informational input into other inventive activities, is especially unlikely to be rewarded. In fact, it is likely to be of commercial value to the firm undertaking it only if other firms are prevented from using the information.

Since the consumption of information by others "does not diminish or degrade it," information, thus, has a propensity to take on the nature of a public good more or less freely available to many consumers (Mowery & Rosenberg, 1989, p. 5). While society may derive significant benefits from the widest possible distribution of information, this approach had the potential to bankrupt the originator of the information.

Clearly, the new marketplace for information demands a guarantee of ownership of the commodity form, and, thus, has at once the potential to limit access to information (only those who can pay can play), and to increase dramatically the creation of new information (entrepreneurs are guaranteed the right to control and sell their "information commodity," and find the incentive to create more of this profitable commodity). Harowitz and Curtis (1984, p. 67) emphasize this point for librarians when they argue for the elimination of the "fair use" exemption in the current copyright law, because it subverts the issue of "fair return." They forcefully insist that

> This issue is not one of limiting use or suppressing information, but of mechanisms for safeguarding the rights of copyright holders . . . and insuring the free flow of information by providing a proper return on both intellectual creativity and capital expenditures.

What now appears necessary is a critical examination of fundamental philosophical and political commitments in the context of these changing times. As a beginning we must critically examine the very purpose of the library in American society.

ESSENTIALLY CONTESTED CONCEPTS: FREEDOM, EQUALITY, NEUTRALITY

Mary Ann Glendon (1991) notes that Americans partake in a peculiar form of "Rights Talk." In a statement that describes both the national approach to the question of rights, and the approach evidenced in the library literature, Glendon (p. x) notes

> It is set apart from rights discourse in other liberal democracies by its starkness and simplicity, its prodigality in bestowing the rights label, its legalistic character, its exaggerated absoluteness, its hyperindividualism, its insularity, and its silence with respect to personal, civic, and collective responsibilities.

While critical of certain aspects of current American "rights talk," she notes that the emergence of an intense and heterogeneous debate about rights like democracy, freedom, and equality occurring as we enter the information era actually promises a redemptive moment in our history. "The ongoing dialogue between freedom and responsibility, individualism and community, present needs and future plans, that takes place daily in a wide variety of American speech communities," she notes, "could help to revitalize our rights tradition as well as our political life" (pp. xii–xiii).

We feel that the current intense debate about the mission of the library in American society shares this same redemptive potential, and that librarians and information professionals should welcome this opportunity to rethink critically and systematically the role of the library in securing and preserving fundamental rights in the post-industrial society. But we also agree with Glendon when she insists that this potential can only be successfully tapped if we are able to transcend our longstanding "disdain for politics," and engage in a sustained and (perhaps) painful form of rights talk of our own.

For library and information professionals this task will not be easy. Anyone familiar with the literature directed at the mission of the library in the post-industrial era will immediately notice that it is heavily "biased by the implicit assumption that technology is an autonomous force with the power to achieve a unilateral impact upon society" (K. Wilson, 1988, p. 3). As such it virtually mitigates against serious rights talk, and proceeds with an apolitical, ahistorical, and decontextualized emphasis on technological determinism, "reckless optimism and reckless despair," that completely overlooks the political economy of library and information services in America. This unfortunate tendency has encouraged librarians to abandon serious philosophical and political argument and, instead, turn to the simpleminded notion that an aggressive mastery of technology will solve all of our problems.

Virtually all serious students of technology development and transfer insist that technology is just one of a number of dependent variables in the institutional mix, and that ultimately people must make deliberate decisions relative to the deployment of technology in the pursuit of institutional objectives and purposes. That is, technology must be seen for what it is, a means toward some institutional end, and we must make conscious our apolitical and wrongheaded conviction that technology development and deployment is an end in itself. Thus, we would argue that any serious attempt to understand the implications of the post-industrial era for library and information service must begin with a serious debate about the mission of library and information services in the United States.

This last chapter of our book will not allow the thorough and critical discussion we suggest. But, one of the objectives of the preceding chapters has been to provide a balanced and critical foundation for such a dialogue. All we can hope to do here is suggest what we see as several promising starting points. First, it should be readily apparent that the general normative consensus on the mission of the library which existed from the late 1940s into the 1970s has now been shattered. We see little benefit in trying to shore up dogmatically the simplistic and absolutist modern remnants of that consensus. Instead, it seems more productive to conclude that fundamental concepts, like "democracy," "freedom," "equality," and "neutrality," have all become "essentially contested concepts." This phrase was first employed by W. B. Gallie (1955–1956), who used the notion to describe "concepts the proper use and meaning of which are the subject of considerable disagreement" (Hanson, 1985, p. 28).

Russell Hanson (1985) notes that arguments over these potent political symbols are considerably more than "linguistic squabbles." In his analysis (p. 29) of the long standing debate over the meaning of arguably the most controversial of the "essentially contested concepts," Hanson writes

> What sets essential contests apart from other linguistic squabbles, however, is the fact that each group's arguments on behalf of its usage of democracy have merit. Indeed, it may even be said that the various group's arguments have more or less *equal* merit, and that no group's usage of democracy is self-evidently superior to any other group's usage. This is because no general principle for evaluating the usages of an essentially contested concept exists. Essentially contested concepts have a uniquely 'open' texture that invites conflicting usages and claims. They are distinguished from other concepts by the fact that they involve the partisan application of multiple criteria, the relative importance of which is unsettled and open to dispute, in the appraisal or evaluation of complex achievements.

And, these achievements, reflecting the "mission" of democracy, when variously interpreted by different partisan groups will result "in different conclusions regarding the praiseworthiness of a given accomplishment" (p. 29). For our purposes, it is apparent that the fundamental philosophical foundations for library and information services in the post-industrial era have once again emerged as "essentially contested concepts" and that the arguments of the various interpreters of these concepts are of "more or less equal merit." Those genuinely concerned with the future of library and information services must recognize the contested and contingent nature of our conceptual underpinnings and confront the reality that insofar as one partisan group is able to establish its definition of, say, democracy as legitimate, they will be able to "institute new practices and legitimate them" (p. 9). That is, they will be able to define the mission of the library. For as the intellectual historian Alastair MacIntyre (1966, pp. 2-3) once observed,

> Since to possess a concept involves behaving or being able to behave in certain ways in certain circumstances, to alter concepts, whether by modifying existing concepts or by making new concepts available or by destroying old ones, is to alter behavior.

In a recent essay, Andrew Ross (1991) discusses the emergence of the "hacker ethic, which . . . asserts the basic right of users to free access to all information." Ross points out that this ethic, developed first by young computer whiz kids at Massachusetts Institute of Technology in the 1950s, was "libertarian and crypto-anarchist in its right-to-know principles" and that the initial reaction to the hackers was to view them as romantic heroes doing battle against corporate power (p. 116). The hacker ethic insisted that centralized control of information was a recipe for fascism, and that information elites were never to be trusted. While the hacker ethic is clearly a radical (and minor) movement in the post-industrial era, it is clear that the ethic's emphasis on the "right-to-know" and its refusal to acknowledge information as a guaranteed commodity form is different in degree, but not in kind, from the approach taken by the American library profession in its official policy statements.

Thus, we find the American Library Association insisting that people have a "right-to-know" and that the idea of access to information trumps all claims based on, for instance, privacy or proprietary issues. However, it is also clear that most Americans do not share this view. The majority would argue that certain matters, especially private matters, are protected from public disclosure and both the courts and the corporate sector have repeatedly demonstrated their belief that no one has a "right-to-know" (or a right to access to) information that is *owned* (copyrighted) by individual or corporate concerns.

Put differently, we might argue that many librarians would insist that freedom (of access to information) demands that all people be given equal access to all information. Others, of course, would insist that freedom of access to information means nothing more than a person's right to maximize his and her utilities by purchasing whatever information he or she deems necessary on a free market. The latter group would insist that nothing is more free, or democratic, than a free marketplace.

Then, there is the intensely contested idea of neutrality. For many of us this idea is interpreted as meaning that we must remain indifferent to the content of the ideas that we collect, preserve, and disseminate—all of this in the service of democracy. That is, we must deliberately remain in Olympian isolation from our sources. For others, the idea of neutrality means that professionals should strive to provide objective but authoritative and prescriptive solutions to client centered problems. By this reading of the word neutrality, librarians must be objective and altruistic, but at the same time must offer discriminating and prescriptive service to clients.

While we do not have the space to work these issues through to any detailed conclusions, it would seem obvious that these ideas are among the "essentially-contested" concepts being so widely debated today. It also seems apparent that if librarians wish to preserve their proud heritage of guaranteeing access to a wide range of information they must acknowledge that their official view is both a contested, and increasingly marginal, element in the current debate about the role of the library in the post-industrial era. Librarians, and their opponents in the information-as-commodity school, must agree to disagree and then turn to serious attempts to argue well about these concepts as they relate to information services in the post-industrial era. While a systematic and principled debate does not guarantee a satisfactory resolution, it surely promises more than what we might expect from the current refusal to even acknowledge the existence of these "essentially contested concepts."

The literature of librarianship is heavily freighted with argument and counter argument relative to the debate about the ability of practicing librarians to effectively reengineer the library to meet the demands of a digital era (Gorman, 1994; Harris & Hannah, 1996). And yet, we find little in that same literature that provides us with a persuasive map of the immediate future.

Perhaps some insight into this dilemma might be gained from a careful analysis of Robert Berring's (1995) essay entitled "Future Librarians." Insisting that we are witnessing a massive paradigm shift in the area of communications, Berring goes on to note that the implications of these changes are disruptive to librarianship (p. 94):

> Whenever a paradigm changes, there are prices to be paid. Paradigm shifts occur when patterns that sorted the old world into recognizable, manageable categories become obstacles preventing an understanding of the new world. The new pattern is difficult to perceive, and the irony is that the tools that aided in understanding the old pattern may obstruct the new. There may be considerable groping toward understanding the nature of the change, which can bring about dislocation, unrest, and fear. Librarians are no different than any other group caught in the midst of such

change. The foundations of librarianship are shaken by the current shift in the information environment, and, indeed, the change is revolutionary.

He goes on to note that such fundamental restructuring will initially lead to quite predictable results. The profession, Berring argues, will split into three basic camps, each with clear-cut ideological tendencies. He defines the three basic ideologies of library service as follows:

- *Conservatives*: In revolutionary times it is the conservatives who plead the truth and the beauty of the old system. They see in the old way a power that will be lost in the face of change. In the change of the information paradigm, the conservatives are the book people, the people who see digital information as part of a general decline in intellectual culture . . . Librarians who are conservatives see themselves as identified with the book, so deeply enmeshed in the world of the book that leaving it destroys the very core of what they do. They resist change in the profession and cling to old explanations of the world. The conservatives view the exponents of change as barbarians pounding upon the gate of the sacred keep.
- *Reformers*: are those who believe that some of the old can sensibly be blended with some of the new to reach the best end. Reformers often share the conservatives' belief that there is some precious kernel in the old way, some style or value that can and must be saved. Yet the reformer also recognizes that the paradigm is changing . . . . Specifically, they feel that society will use both books and digital information in the future.
- *Radicals*: are the true believers in total change. They see the old system as a problem in and of itself. For them it is time to shed the skin of the old system . . . . They see the reformers as especially feckless; for the radical, half measures have no place . . . For librarians, the radicals are represented by those who feel that the entire template of librarianship must be discarded . . . . Indeed, radicals may see themselves as no longer associated with librarianship at all as they attempt to create a new reality for the profession (p. 95).

Berring's analysis provides a useful topography of the current culture wars in American librarianship. However, if Berring is right and many librarians are conservatives, "the book people," and if very few "radicals" view the profession as a hospitable environment, the profession could be severely retarded in its attempt to forge a new future for library and information service in the digital era.

What is vital now is the recognition that a commitment to arguing well is essential for the preservation and development of the significant traditional role of libraries in American society. Librarians and information professionals should not seek premature and forced closure to the debate, but rather should dedicate themselves to an "extended argument" that will preserve and enlarge past accomplishments while at the same time recognizing the merits of contending arguments and their role in the definition of the mission of the library in the post-industrial era (Hanson, 1985, p. 33). Rather than fearing debate on fundamental conceptual foundations we might read the current flurry of philosophical argument about the mission of the library as reasoned "responses to, reflections upon, and antidotes for conceptual chaos and communicative breakdown" (Ball, Farr, & Hanson, 1989, p. 2). In short, we must recognize that "political words," like freedom and equality, represent "contested terrain" and probably always will (Rodgers, 1987).

Librarians and information professionals must struggle to establish a consensus on these contested concepts as a preliminary to establishing a widespread agreement on the mission of the profession in the post-industrial world. Without such a philosophical and jurisdictional quest, the new information professionals may well know how to do what they do, but they will lack the fundamental sense of mission that must guide the deployment of their technical skills.

References

Abbott, A. (1988). *The system of professions: An essay on the division of expert labor*. Chicago: University of Chicago Press.

Adams, J. A. (1988). The computer catalog: A democratic or authoritarian technology? *Library Journal, 113*, 31–36.

Agger, B. (1989). *Fast capitalism: A critical theory of significance*. Urbana: University of Illinois Press.

Alford, R. R., & Friedland, R. (1985). *Powers of theory: Capitalism, the state, and democracy*. Cambridge, U.K.: Cambridge University Press.

Allen, T. J., & Morton, M. S. (Eds.) (1994). *Information technology and the corporation of the 1990s: Research studies*. Oxford: Oxford University Press.

Apostle, R., & Raymond, B. (1986). Librarianship and the information paradigm. *Canadian Library Journal, 43*, 377–384.

Archer, M. (1990). Theory, culture and post-industrial society. In M. Featherstone (Ed.), *Global culture: Nationalism, globalization and modernity*, (pp. 97–120). London: Sage.

Arendt, H. (1951). *The origins of totalitarianism*. New York: Harcourt, Brace.

Aronowitz, S., & DiFazio, W. (1994). *The jobless future: Sci-Tech and the dogma of work*. Minneapolis: University of Minnesota Press.

Artandi, S. (1979). Man, information, and society: New patterns of interaction. *Journal of the American Society for Information Science, 30*, 15–18.

Asheim, L. (1978). Librarians as professionals. *Library Trends, 26*, 225–257.

Asheim, L. (1982). Ortega revisited. *Library Quarterly, 52*, 215–226.

Association of Research Libraries. (1995). *Copyright, public policy and the scholarly community*. Washington, DC.

Attewell, P. (1987). The deskilling controversy. *Work and Occupations, 14*, 323–346.

Badham, R. (1984). The sociology of industrial and post-industrial societies. *Current Sociology, 32*, 1–141.

Baethge, M., & Oberbeck, H. (1989). The future of the white collar worker. In H. Ernste & C. Jaeger (Eds.), *Information society and spatial structure*, (pp. 117–129). London: Belhaven Press.

Ball, T., Farr, J. & Hanson, R. L. (Eds.). (1989). *Political innovation and conceptual change*. Cambridge, U.K.: Cambridge University Press.

Barber, B. (1984). *Strong democracy: Participatory politics for a new age*. Berkeley: University of California Press.

Barglow, R. (1994). *The crisis of the self in the age of information*. London: Routledge.

Barrett, E. (Ed.) (1992). *Sociomedia: Multimedia, hypermedia, and the social construction of knowledge*. Cambridge, MA: MIT Press.

Beard, M. (1990, February 8). Cleopatra's books. *London Review of Books*, 11.

Bell, D. (1960). *The end of ideology: On the exhaustion of political ideas in the fifties*. Glencoe, IL: Free Press.

Bell, D. (1967a). Notes on the post-industrial society. *Public Interest*, 6–7, 24–35; 102–118.

Bell, D. (Ed.). (1967b). Toward the year 2000: Work in progress. *Daedalus, 96*, whole issue.

Bell, D. (1973a). *The coming of post-industrial society: A venture in social forecasting*. New York: Basic Books.

Bell, D. (1973b). A rejoinder (to Tilton). *Social Research, 40*, 745–752.

Bell, D. (1974a). Reply to Peter Sterns. *Society, 11*, 23–25.

Bell, D. (1974b). Twelve modes of prediction. In A. Somit (Ed.), *Political science and the study of the future*, (pp. 40–67). Hinsdale, IL: Dryden Press.

Bell, D. (1976). *The cultural contradictions of capitalism*. New York: Basic Books.

Bell, D. (1977). The "intelligensia" in American society. In S. Sandmel (Ed.), *Tomorrow's American* (pp. 23–46). Oxford: Oxford University Press.

Bell, D. (1979). The new class: A muddled concept. In R. Bruce-Briggs (Ed.), *The new class? America's educated elite examined* (pp. 169–190). New York: McGraw-Hill.

Bell, D. (1980a). The social framework of the information society. In T. Forester (Ed.), *The microelectronics revolution: The complete guide to the new technology and its impact on society*, (pp. 500–549). Cambridge, MA: MIT.

Bell, D. (1980b). Teletext and technology: New networks of knowledge and information in postindustrial society. In D. Bell (Ed.),*Winding passage: Essays and sociological journeys* (pp. 34–66). New York: Basic Books.

Bell, D. (1982). Mr. Veysey's strabismus. *American Quarterly, 34*, 82–87.

Bell, D. (1985). Gutenberg & the computer: On information, knowledge & other distinctions. *Encounter, 64*, 15–20.

Bell, D. (1987). The world and the United States in 2013. *Daedalus, 116*, 1–31.

Bell, D. (1989). The third technological revolution. *Dissent, 36*, 164–176.

Bendix, R. (1974). Review of D. Bell *The Coming of Post-Industrial Society*. *Contemporary Sociology, 3*, 99–101.

Beniger, J. (1986). *The control revolution: Technological and economic origins of the information society*. Cambridge, MA: Harvard University Press.

Berninghausen, D. (1979). Intellectual freedom in librarianship: Advances and retreats. *Advances in Librarianship, 9*, 1–29.

Berring, R. C. (1995). Future librarians. In R. H. Bloch & C. Hesse (Eds.), *Future Libraries* (pp. 94–115). Berkeley: University of California Press.

Berry, J. (1979). Introduction: Information ideology. *Library journal, 104*, 1731–1733.

Bijker, W. E., Hughes, T. P., & Pinch, T. (Eds.). (1987). *The social construction of technological systems*. Cambridge, MA: MIT Press.

Bijker, W. E., & Law, J. (Eds.). (1992). *Shaping technology/Building society.* Cambridge, MA: MIT Press.

Birdsall, W. F. (1982). Librarianship, professionalism, & social change. *Library Journal, 107,* 223–226.

Birdsall, W. F. (1994). *The myth of the electronic library: Librarianship and social change in America.* New York: Greenwood Press.

Birkerts, S. (1994). *The Gutenberg elegies: The fate of reading in an electronic age.* Boston: Faber and Faber.

Blackstone, W. (1979). *Commentaries on the laws of England.* A facsimile of the first edition of 1765–69. Chicago: University of Chicago Press.

Blake, F. M. (1978). Let my people know: Access to information in a postindustrial society. *Wilson Library Bulletin, 52,* 392–399.

Blanke, H. T. (1989). Librarianship & political values: Neutrality or commitment? *Library Journal, 114,* 39–43.

Blanke, H. T. (1990-91). Libraries and the commercialization of information: Towards a critical discourse of librarianship. *Progressive Librarian, 2,* 9–14.

Bloch, R. H., & Hesse, C. (Eds.). (1995). *Future libraries.* Berkeley: University of California Press.

Block, F. (1987). *Revising state theory: Essays in politics and postindustrialism.* Philadelphia, PA: Temple University Press.

Block, F. (1990). *Postindustrial possibilities: A critique of economic discourse.* Berkeley: University of California Press.

Bok, D. (1986). *Higher learning.* Cambridge, MA: Harvard University Press.

Bolter, J. D. (1984). *Turing's man: Western culture in the computer age.* Chapel Hill: University of North Carolina.

Bolter, J. D. (1991). *Writing space: The computer, hypertext, and the history of writing.* Hillsdale, NJ: Lawrence Erlbaum Associates.

Boorstin, D. J. (1982). Gresham's law: Knowledge or information. *Antiquarian Bookman, 69,* 1379–1388.

Bowers, C. A. (1988). *The cultural dimensions of educational computing: Understanding the non-neutrality of technology.* New York: Teachers College Press.

Bowes, J. E. (1981). Japan's approach to an information society: A critical perspective. *Keio Communication Review, 2,* 39–49.

Bowles, S., & Gintis, H. (1986). *Democracy and capitalism: Property, community, and the contradictions of modern social thought.* New York: Basic Books.

Boyett, J. H., & Conn, H. P. (1992). *Workplace 2000: The revolution reshaping American business.* London: Penguin Books.

Boyle, J. (1996). *Shamans, software, and spleens: Law and the construction of the information society.* Chapel Hill: University of North Carolina Press.

Branscomb, A. W. (1994). *Who owns information? From privacy to public access.* New York: Basic Books.

Branscomb, A. W. (1995, Dec.-Jan.). Public and private domains of information: Defining the legal boundaries. *Bulletin of the American Society for Information Science,* 14–18.

Branscomb, L. M. (Ed.). (1993). *Empowering technology: Implementing a U. S. strategy.* Cambridge, MA: MIT Press.

Brants, K. (1989). The social construction of the information revolution. *European Journal of Communication, 4*, 79–97.

Braverman, H. (1974). *Labor and monopoly capital: The degradation of work in the twentieth century.* New York: Monthly Review Press.

Braverman, M. (1982). From Adam Smith to Ronald Reagan: Public libraries as a public good. *Library Journal, 107*, 397–401.

Brint, S. (1994). *In an age of experts: The changing role of professionals in politics and public life.* Princeton, NJ: Princeton University Press.

Brook, J., & Boal, I. A. (Eds.). (1995). *Resisting the virtual life: The culture and politics of information.* San Francisco, CA: City Lights.

Brown, R. D. (1996). *The strength of a people: The idea of an informed citizenry in America, 1650-1870.* Chapel Hill: University of North Carolina Press.

Bruce-Briggs, B. (Ed.). (1979). *The new class: America's educated elite examined.* New York: McGraw-Hill.

Bruchey, S. (1990). *Enterprise: The dynamic economy of a free people.* Cambridge, MA: Harvard University Press.

Buckland, M. K. (1988). *Library services in theory and context* (2nd ed.). Oxford, U.K.: Pergamon Press.

Budd, J. (1995-1996, Winter). Technology and library and information science. *Progressive Librarian*, 43–59.

Budd, J., & Seavey, C. A. (1996). Productivity of U.S. library and information science faculty: The Hayes report revisited. *Library Quarterly, 66*, 1–20.

Bundy, M. L., & Wasserman, P. (1968). Professionalism reconsidered. *College & Research Libraries, 29*, 5–26.

Bundy, M. L., & Stielow, F. (Eds.). (1987). *Activism in American librarianship, 1962-73.* Westport, CT.: Greenwood Press.

Burris, B. H. (1989). Technocracy and gender in the workplace. *Social Problems, 36*, 165–80.

Burstein, D., & Kline, D. (1995). *Road warriors: Dreams and nightmares along the information highway.* New York: Dutton.

Buschman, J. (1990). Asking the right questions about information technology. *American Libraries, 21*, 1026–1030.

Buschman, J. (Ed.). (1993). *Critical approaches to information technology in librarianship.* Westport, CT: Greenwood Press.

Buschman, J. (1995). Libraries and the underside of the information age. *Libri, 45*, 209–215.

Buschman, J., & Carbone, M. (1991). A critical inquiry into librarianship: Applications of the "new sociology of education." *Library Quarterly, 61*, 15–40.

Butler, P. (1933). *Introduction to library science.* Chicago: University of Chicago Press.

Butler, P. (1951). Librarianship as a profession. *Library Quarterly, 21*, 235–247.

Campbell, J. D. (1993, June). Choosing to have a future. *American Libraries*, 560–566.

Carey, J. W. (1984). The paradox of the book. *Library Trends, 33*, 103–113.

Carey, J. W. (1989). The mythos of the electronic revolution. In J. W. Carey (Ed.), *Communication as culture: Essays on media and society* (pp. 113–141). Boston: Unwin Hyman.

Carnoy, M. (1984). *The state and political theory.* Princeton, NJ: Princeton University Press.

Carrigan, D. (1990). The political economy of scholarly communication and the American system of higher education. *Journal of Academic Librarianship, 15,* 332–337.

Carrigan, D. (1991). Publish or perish: The troubled state of scholarly communication. *Scholarly Publishing, 22,* 131–142.

Carroll, B. A. (1990). The politics of "originality": Women and the class system of the intellect. *Journal of Women's History, 2,* 136–163.

Carter, D. H. (1981). The library charter: Is it time for a rewrite? *Library Journal, 106,* 1385–1386.

Christian-Smith, L. K. (1991). Texts and high tech: Computers, gender, and book publishing. In M. Apple & L. Christian-Smith (Eds.), *The politics of the textbook,* (pp. 41–55). London: Routledge.

Cockburn, C. (1988). *Machinery of dominance: Women, men, and technical know-how.* Boston: Northeastern University Press.

Code, L. (1991). *What can she know? Feminist theory and the construction of knowledge.* Ithaca, NY: Cornell University Press.

Coleman, J. S. (1982). *The asymmetric society.* Syracuse, NY: Syracuse University Press.

Crawford, W., & Gorman, M. (1995). *Future libraries: Dreams, madness and reality.* Chicago: American Library Association.

Crews, K. D. (1993). *Copyright, fair use and the challenge for universities.* Chicago: University of Chicago Press.

Cronin, B. (1983). Adaptation, extinction or genetic drift? *Aslib Procedings, 35,* 278–289.

Curley, A. (1994, July/August). Libraries: An American value. *American Libraries ,* 691.

Czitrom, D. M. (1982). *Media and the American mind from morse to McLuhan.* Chapel Hill: University of North Carolina Press.

Dalhgren, P. (1987). Ideology and information in the public sphere. In J. Slack & F. Fejes (Eds.), *The ideology of the information age,* (pp. 24–45). Norwood, NJ: Ablex.

DeGennaro, R. (1985). Integrated online library systems: Perspectives, perceptions, and practicalities. *Library Journal, 110,* 37–40.

Demac, D. A. (1990). New communication technologies: A plug'n'play world? In J. Downing (Ed.), *Questioning the media: A critical introduction,* (pp. 207–216). Newbury Park, CA.: Sage.

Derber, C., Schwartz, W., & Magrass, Y. (1990). *Power in the highest degree: Professionals and the rise of a new mandarin order.* Oxford, U.K.: Oxford University Press.

Dervin, B. (1994). Information/democracy: An examination of the underlying assumptions. *Journal of the American Society for Information Science, 45,* 369–385.

Detlefsen, E. (1984). User costs: Information as a social good vs. information as a commodity. *Government Publications Review, 11,* 385–394.

Doeringer, P. B. (1991). *Turbulence in the American workplace.* Oxford, U.K.: Oxford University Press.

Donahue, J. D. (1989). *The privatization decision: Public ends, private means.* New York: Basic Books.

Dougherty, R. D. (1991). An ideal win-win situation: The national electronic highway. *American Libraries, 22,* 182.

Dowlin, K. E. (1980). The electronic eclectic library. *Library Journal, 105,* 2265–2270.

Dudley, K.M. (1994). *The end of the line: Lost jobs, new lives in postindustrial America.* Chicago: University of Chicago Press.

Duncan, G. (Ed.). (1989). *Democracy and the capitalist state*. Cambridge, U.K.: Cambridge University Press.

Durkheim, E. (1984). *The division of labor in society*. Trans. W. D. Halls. New York: Free Press.

Ehrenreich, B. (1989). *Fear of falling: The inner life of the middle class*. New York: Harper.

Ekecrantz, J. (1987). The sociological order of the new information society. In J. Slack & F. Fejes (Eds.), *The ideology of the information age*, (pp. 78–94). Norwood, NJ: Ablex.

Ellul, J. (1964). *The technological society*. New York: Vintage.

Ellul, J. (1990). *The technological bluff*. Grand Rapids, MI: Eerdmans Publishing.

Epstein, J. (1990). The decline and rise of publishing. *New York Review of Books, 37*, 8–12.

Epstein, S. B. (1991). Turnkey or software-only? *Library Journal, 116*, 168–171.

Erikson, K., & Vallas, S. P. (Eds.). (1990). *The nature of work: Sociological perspectives*. New Haven, CT: Yale University Press.

Estabrook, L. (Ed.). (1977). *Libraries in postindustrial society*. Phoenix, AZ: Oryx Press.

Estabrook, L. (1981a). Labor & librarians: The divisiveness of professionalism. *Library Journal, 106*, 125–27.

Estabrook, L. (1981b). Productivity, profit, and libraries. *Library Journal, 106*, 1377–1380.

Estabrook, L., (1984). Women's work in the library/information sector. In K. Sacks & D. Remy (Eds.), *My troubles are going to have trouble with me: Everyday trials and triumphs of women workers*, (pp. 160-172). New Brunswick, NJ: Rutgers University Press.

Estabrook, L. (1989). The growth of the profession. *College & Research Libraries, 50*, 287–296.

Evans, P. B., Rueschemeyer, D., & Skocpol, T. (Eds.). (1985). *Bringing the state back in*. Cambridge, U.K.: Cambridge University Press.

Fallows, J. (1996, Feb. 15). Caught in the web. *New York Review of Books*, 17–18.

Fayen, E. G. (1986). Beyond technology: Rethinking "librarian." *American Libraries, 17*, 240–242.

Feenberg, A. (1991). *Critical theory of technology*. Oxford, U.K.: Oxford University Press.

Feenberg, A. (1995). *Alternative modernity: The technical turn in philosophy and social theory*. Berkeley: University of California Press.

Feenberg, A., & Hannay, A. (Eds.). (1995). *Technology and the politics of knowledge*. Bloomington: Indiana University Press.

Ferkiss, V. (1979). Daniel Bell's concept of post-industrial society: Theory, myth and ideology. *Political Science Reviewer, 9*, 61–102.

Forester, T. (1989). Editor's introduction: Making sense of IT. In T. Forester (Ed.), *Computers in the human context: Information technology, productivity, and people* (pp. 1–15). Cambridge, MA: MIT Press.

Form, W. (1987). On the degradation of skills. *Annual Review of Sociology* 13, 29–47.

Fox, R. W. (1982). Breathless: The cultural consternation of Daniel Bell. *American Quarterly, 34*, 70–77.

Frankel, B. (1987). *The post-industrial utopians*. Madison: University of Wisconsin Press.

Fraser, S. (1995). *The bell curve wars*. New York: Basic Books.

Freidson, E. (1986). *Professional powers: A study of the institutionalization of formal knowledge.* Chicago: University of Chicago Press.

Freidson, E. (1994). *Professionalism reborn: Theory, prophecy and policy.* Chicago: University of Chicago Press.

Friedman, M. (1979). The economics of free speech. In B. Siegan (Ed.), *Regulation, economics and the law.* Lexington, MA: D. C. Heath.

Fromm, H. (1991). *Academic capitalism & literary value.* Athens: University of Georgia Press.

Fuller, P. F. (1994). The politics of LSCA during the Reagan and Bush administrations: An analysis. *Library Quarterly, 64,* 294–318.

Gallie, W. B. (1955–56). Essentially contested concepts. *Proceedings of the Aristotelian Society, 56,* 167–198.

Gandy, O. H., Jr. (1982). *Beyond agenda setting: Information subsidies and public policy.* Norwood, NJ: Ablex.

Gandy, O. H. (1993). *The panoptic sort: A political economy of personal information.* Boulder, CO: Westview Press.

Garceau, O. (1949). *The public library in the political process.* New York: Columbia University Press.

Garson, B. (1988). *The electronic sweatshop: How computers are transforming the office of the future into the factory of the past.* New York: Penguin.

Garver, E. (1978). Rhetoric and essentially contested arguments. *Philosophy and Rhetoric, 11,* 156–172.

Gates, B. (1995). *The road ahead.* New York: Viking.

Gaughan, T. (1995, January). ALA goal 2000: Planning for the millenium. *American Libraries,* 17–21.

Gell, M. K. (1979). The politics of information. *Library Journal, 104,* 1735–1738.

Geller, E. (1984). *Forbidden books in American public libraries, 1876–1939: A study in cultural change.* Westport, CT: Greenwood Press.

Gillam, R. (1982). The perils of postindustrialism. *American Quarterly, 34,* 77–82.

Ginzberg, E., Noyelle, T., & Stanback, T. (1986). *Technology and employment: Concepts and clarifications.* Boulder, CO: Westview.

Giuliano, V. E. (1978). *Into the information age: A perspective for federal action on information.* Chicago: American Library Association.

Givens, B. (1995, May). Aunt Ruth's trunk: A futuristic scenario about the information rich-poor gap. *American Libraries,* 414–416.

Glendon, M. A. (1991). *Rights talk: The impovrishment of political discourse.* New York: Free Press.

Golding, P., & Murdock, G. (1986). Unequal information: Access and exclusion in the new communications market place. In M. Ferguson (Ed.), *New communication technologies and the public interest* (pp. 71–83). London: Sage.

Goode, W. J. (1962). The librarian: from occupation to profession? In P. Ennis & H. Winger (Eds.), *Seven questions about the profession of librarianship* (pp. 8–22). Chicago: University of Chicago Press.

Gorman, M. (1991). Scholarship, teaching and libraries in an electronic age. *Library Hi Tech, 9,* 73–75.

Gorman, M. (1994, Feb. 15). The treason of the learned: The real agenda of those who would destroy libraries and books. *Library Journal,* 130–31.

Gouldner, A. W. (1979). *The future of intellectuals and the rise of the new class*. New York: Seabury Press.

Graff, H. J. (1987). *The legacies of literacy: Continuities and contradictions in Western culture and society*. Bloomington: Indiana University Press.

Gremmels, G. S. (1991). Reference in the public interest: An examination of ethics. *RQ, 30*, 362–369.

Grimm, J. W. (1988). Women in female-dominated professions. In A. Stromberg & S. Harkness (Eds.), *Women working: Theories and facts in perspective* (pp. 293–315). Palo Alto, CA: Mayfield.

Grint, K. (1991). *The sociology of work: An introduction*. Cambridge, MA: Polity Press.

Hammer, D. P. (Ed.). (1976). *The information age: Its development, its impact*. Metuchen, NJ: Scarecrow Press.

Handlin, O. (1987). Libraries and learning. *American Scholar, 56*, 205–218.

Hanson, R. L. (1985). *The democratic imagination in America: Conversations with our past*. Princeton, NJ: Princeton University Press.

Harris, M. H. (1976). Portrait in paradox: Commitment and ambivalence in American librarianship. *Libri, 26*, 281–301.

Harris, M. H. (1986a). State, class, and cultural reproduction: Toward a theory of library service in the United States. *Advances in Librarianship, 14*, 211–252.

Harris, M. H. (1986b). The dialectic of defeat: Antinomies in research in library and information science. *Library Trends, 34*, 515–531.

Harris, M. H. (1991, Nov.). [Political economy of scholarly production]: A letter to the editor. *College & Research Libraries*, 586.

Harris, M. H. (1992, Summer). No love lost: Library women vs. women who use libraries. *Progressive Librarian*, 1–18.

Harris, M. H. (1995a). *History of libraries in the western world* (4th ed.). Metuchen, NJ: Scarecrow Press.

Harris, M. H. (1995b). The fall of the grand hotel: Class, canon, and the coming crisis of western librarianship. *Libri, 45*, 231–235.

Harris, M. H. (1996). Review of *The Bell Curve*. *Library Quarterly, 66*, 89–92.

Harris, M. H., & Carrigan, D. (1990). The President and library policy. In E. J. Josey & K. Shearer (Eds.), *Politics and the support of libraries* (pp. 32–42). New York: Neal-Schuman.

Harris, M. H., & Hannah, S. A. (1992). Why do we study the history of libraries: A meditiation on the perils of ahistoricism in the post-industrial era. *Journal of Research in Library and Information Science, 14*, 123–130.

Harris, M. H., & Hannah, S. A. (1996, Jan.). The treason of the librarians: Core communication technologies and opportunity costs in the information era. *Journal of Academic Librarianship*, 3–8.

Harris, M. H., & Itoga, M. (1991). Becoming critical: For a theory of purpose and necessity in American librarianship. In C. R. McClure & P. Hernon (Eds.), *Library & information science research* (pp. 347–57). Norwood, NJ: Ablex.

Harris, M. H., & Tourjee, M. (1983). William S. Dix. In W. Wiegand (Ed.), *Leaders in American academic librarianship, 1925–75* (pp. 50–71). Pittsburgh, PA: Beta Phi Mu.

Harris, R. M. (1992). *Librarianship: The erosion of a woman's profession*. Norwood, NJ: Ablex.

Harris, R. M. (1993, Oct.). Gender, power, and the dangerous pursuit of professionalism. *American Libraries*, 874–876.

Harris, R. M. (1995–1996, Winter). Service undermined by technology: Gender relations, economics and ideology. *Progressive Librarian*, 5–22.

Haug, M.R. (1977). Computer technology and the obsolescence of the concept of the profession. In M. R. Haug & J. Domy (Eds.), *Work and technology* (pp. 215–228). Beverly Hills, CA: Sage.

Hayes, R. (1983). Citation statistics as a measure of faculty research productivity. *Journal of Education for Librarianship, 23*, 151–172.

Head, S. (1996, Feb.). The new, ruthless economy. *New York Review of Books*, 47–52.

Heidegger, M. (1977). *The question concerning technology and other essays*. New York: Harper and Row.

Heim, K. (1986). National information policy and a mandate for oversight by the information professions. *Government Publications Review, 13*, 21–37.

Heim, M. (1987). *Electronic language: A philosophical study of word processing*. New Haven, CT: Yale University Press.

Heim, M. (1993). *The metaphysics of virtual reality*. Oxford: Oxford University Press.

Henig, J. R. (1989-1990). Privatization in the United States: Theory and practice. *Political Science Quarterly, 104*, 649–670.

Henig, J. R. 1994. *Rethinking school choice: Limits of the market metaphor*. Princeton: Princeton University Press.

Henry, C. (1994, Dec.). On the necessity of a networked cultural heritage. *Wilson Library Bulletin*, 21–23.

Hernon, P., McClure, C. R., & Relyea, H. (1996). *Federal information policies in the 1990's: Views and perspectives*. Norwood, NJ: Ablex.

Herrnstein, R. J., & Murray, C. (1994). *The Bell curve*. New York: The Free Press.

Herron, J. (1988). *Universities and the myth of cultural decline*. Detroit: Wayne State University Press.

Hesse, C. (1996). Books in time. In G. Nunberg (Ed.), *The future of the book* (pp. 21–36). Berkeley: University of California Press.

Higonnet, P. (1991, August 15). Scandal on the Seine. *New York Review of Books*, 32–33.

Hirschhorn, L. (1984). *Beyond mechanization: Work and technology in a post-industrial age*. Cambridge, MA: MIT Press.

Hirschman, A. O. (1991). *The rhetoric of reaction: Perversity, futility, jeopardy*. Cambridge, MA: Harvard University Press.

Hoesterey, I. (Ed.). (1991). *Zeitgeist in Babel: The post-modernist controversy*. Bloomington: Indiana University Press.

Horowitz, I. L. (1991). *Communicating ideas: The politics of scholarly publishing* (2nd ed.). New Brunswick, NJ: Transaction Publishers.

Horowitz, I. L., & Curtis, M. E. (1984). Fair use versus fair return: Copyright legislation and its consequences. *Journal of the American Society for Information Science, 35*, 67–74.

Hughes, K. D. (1996). Transformed by technology? The changing nature of women's "traditional" and "nontraditional" white collar work. *Work, Employment and Society, 10*, 227–250.

Ivy, M. (1988). Critical texts, mass artifacts: The consumption of knowledge in Postmodern Japan. *The South Atlantic Quarterly, 87*, 419–444.

Jacobs, J. A. (1989). *Revolving doors: Sex segregation and women's careers.* Stanford, CA: Stanford University Press.

Jacoby, R., & Glauberman, N. (Eds.). (1995). *The Bell curve debate.* New York: Times Books.

Jameson, F. (1991). *Postmodernism: or, The cultural logic of late capitalism.* Durham, NC: Duke University Press.

Jansen, S. C. (1989). Gender and the information society: A socially structured silence. *Journal of Communication, 39,* 196–215.

Jensen, J. (1990). *Redeeming modernity: Contradictions in media criticism.* Newbury Park, CA: Sage.

John, R. R. (1995). *Spreading the news: The American postal system from franklin to morse.* Cambridge, MA: Harvard University Press.

Johnson, M. F., Jr. (1982). After the online catalog: A call for active librarianship. *American Libraries, 13,* 235–239.

Jones, B. (1982). *Sleepers wake: Technology & the future of work.* Oxford, U.K.: Oxford University Press.

Josey, E. J. (Ed.). (1978). *The information society: Issues and answers.* Phoenix, AZ: Oryx Press.

Kadushin, C. (1974). *The American intellectual elite.* Boston: Little, Brown.

Kahin, B., & Keller, J. (1995). *Public access to the internet.* Cambridge, MA: MIT Press.

Katch, M. E. (1995). *Law in a digital world.* Oxford, U.K.: Oxford University Press.

Keen, P. G. W. (1991). *Shaping the future: Business design through information technology.* Boston: Harvard Business Press.

Kielbowicz, R. B. (1989). *News in the mail: The press, post office and public information, 1700–1860s.* New York: Greenwood Press.

Kiesler, S., Sproull, L., & Eccles, J. S. (1985). Pool halls, chips, and war games: Women in the culture of computing. *Psychology of Women Quarterly, 9,* 451–462.

King, R. F. (1993). *Money, time and politics: Investment tax subsidies and American democracy.* New Haven, CT: Yale University Press.

Kling, R., (ed.). (1995). *Computerization and controversy: Value conflicts and social Choices.* San Diego, CA: Academic Press.

Kling, R., & Lamb, R. (1996). Analyzing alternate visions of electronic publishing and digital libraries. In R. P. Peek & G. B. Newby (Eds.), *Scholarly publishing: The electronic frontier* (pp. 17–54). Cambridge, MA: MIT Press.

Kraft, P. (1979). The industrialization of computer programming. In A. Zimbalist (Ed.), *Case studies on the labor process* (pp. 1–17). New York: Monthly Review Press.

Kraemer, K. L. (1991). Strategic computing and administrative reform. In C. Dunlop & R. Kling (Eds.), *Computerization and controversy: Value conflicts and social choices* (pp. 150–166). San Diego, CA: Academic Press.

Kramer, P. E., & Lehman, S. (1990). Mismeasuring women: A critique of research on computer ability and avoidance. *Signs, 16,* 158–172.

Kronick, D. A. (1982). GoodBye to farewells: Resource sharing and cost sharing. *Journal of Academic Librarianship, 8,* 132–136.

Kuhn, T. S. (1970). *The stucture of scientific revolutions.* (2nd ed.). Chicago: University of Chicago Press.

Kumar, K. (1978). *Prophesy and progress: The sociology of industrial and post-industrial society.* New York: Penguin.

Kumar, K. (1995). *From post-industrial to post-modern*. Oxford: Blackwell.

Kuttner, R. (1997). *The virtues and limits of markets*. New York: Knopf.

Lacy, D. (1978). Liberty and knowledge, then and now: 1776–1876–1976. In H. Goldstein (Ed.), *Milestones to the present* (pp. 7–52). Syracuse, NY: Gaylord.

Lancaster, F. W. (1978a). Whither libraries? Or, wither libraries? *College & Research Libraries, 39*, 345–357.

Lancaster, F. W. (1978b). *Toward paperless information systems*. New York: Academic Press.

Lancaster, F. W. (1980a). Libraries and the information age. *ALA Yearbook, 5*, 9–19.

Lancaster, F. W. (1980b). Future of the Librarian lies outside of the library. *Catholic Library World, 51*, 388–391.

Lancaster, F. W. (1982a). The future of libraries in the age of telecommunications. In R.E. Hoover (Ed.), *Changing information concepts and technologies* (pp. 137–156). White Plains, NY: Knowledge Industries.

Lancaster, F. W. (1982b). *Libraries and librarians in an age of electronics*. Arlington, VA: Information Resources Press.

Lancaster, F. W. (1983). Future librarianship: Preparing for an unconventional career. *Wilson Library Bulletin, 57*, 747–753.

Lancaster, F. W. (1985). The paperless society revisited. *American Libraries, 16*, 553–555.

Lancaster, F. W. (1991a). Has technology failed us? In A. H. Helal & J. W. Weiss (Eds.), *Information technology and library management* (pp. 2–13). Essen, Germany: Universitatsbibliothek Essen.

Lancaster, F. W. (1991b). *Indexing and abstracting in theory and practice*. Champaign: University of Illinois Graduate School of Library and Information Science.

Lancaster, F. W. (Ed.). (1995). Networked scholarly publishing. *Library Trends, 43*, 515–770.

Lancaster, F. W., Drasgow, L. S., & Marks, E. B. (1980). The role of the library in an electronic society. In F. W. Lancaster *The role of the library in an electronic society: Proceedings of the sixteenth annual clinic on library applications of data processing*, (pp. 162–189). Urbana: University of Illinois, Graduate School of Library and Information Science.

Landauer, T. K. (1995). *The trouble with computers: Usefulness, usability, and productivity*. Cambridge, MA: MIT Press.

Landow, G. P. (1992). *Hypertext: The convergence of contemporary critical theory and technology*. Cambridge, MA: MIT Press.

Landow, G. P. (Ed.). (1994). *Hyper/Text/Theory*. Baltimore: Johns Hopkins University Press.

Lanham, R. A. (1993). *The electronic word: Democracy, technology, and the arts*. Chicago: University of Chicago Press.

Larsen, S. (1988). The idea of an electronic library: A critical essay. *Libri, 38*, 159–177.

Larson, M. S. (1977). *The rise of professionalism: A sociological analysis*. Berkeley: University of California Press.

Lasch, C. (1991). *The true and only heaven: Progress and its critics*. New York: Norton.

Lauter, P. (1991). *Canons and contexts*. Oxford: Oxford University Press.

Leiss, W. (1989). The myth of the Information Society. In I. Angus & S. Jhally (Eds.), *Cultural Politics in Contemporary America*, (pp. 282–298). New York: Routledge.

Levinson, P. (1989). Intelligent writing: The electronic liberation of text. *Technology in Society, 11*, 387–400.

Licklider, J. C. R. (1965). *Libraries of the future.* Cambridge, MA: MIT Press.

Liebowitz, N. (1985). *Daniel Bell and the agony of modern liberalism.* Westport, CT: Greenwood Press.

Line, M. B. (1981). Libraries and information services in a post-technological society. *Journal of Library Automation, 14*, 252–267.

Linowes, D. (1988). *Privatization: Toward more effective government: Report of the President's commission on privatization.* Urbana: University of Illinois Press.

Lubar, S. (1993). *Infoculture: The Smithsonian book of information age inventions.* Boston: Houghton Mifflin Company.

Luke, T. W. (1989). *Screens of power: Ideology, domination, and resistance in informational society.* Urbana: University of Illinois Press.

Lyotard, J. F. (1984). *The postmodern condition: A report on knowledge.* Minneapolis: University of Minnesota Press.

McCain, R. A. (1988). Information as property and as a public good: Perspectives from the economic theory of property rights. *Library Quarterly, 58*, 265–282.

McCook, K. D. (1993, July/August). The first virtual reality. *Library Journal* (July/August), 626–628.

McFarlan, F. W. (1984). Information technology changes the way you compete. *Harvard Business Review, 62*, 98–103.

Machlup, F. (1962). *The production and distribution of knowledge in the United States.* Princeton, NJ: Princeton University Press.

Machlup, F. (1980). *Knowledge: Its creation, distribution and economic significance. (Vol. 1. Knowledge and Knowledge Production).* Princeton, NJ: Princeton University Press.

Machlup, F. (1982). *Knowledge: Its creation, distribution and economic significance. (Vol. II: The Branches of Learning).* Princeton, NJ: Princeton University Press.

Machlup, F. 1984. *Knowledge: Its creation, distribution and economic significance. (Vol. III: The Economics of Information and Human Capital).* Princeton, NJ: Princeton University Press.

MacIntyre, A. (1966). *A short history of ethics.* New York: Macmillan.

Main, L. (1990). Research versus practice: A "No" contest. *Journal of Education for Library and Information Science, 30*, 226–228.

Manguel, A. (1996). *A history of reading.* New York: Viking.

Martin, H. (1994). *The history and power of writing.* Chicago: University of Chicago Press.

Marvin, C. (1987). Information and history. In J. Slack & F. Fejes (Eds.), *The ideology of the information age* (pp. 49–62). Norwood, NJ: Ablex.

Mason, R. O. (1990). What is an information professional? *Journal of Education for Library and Information Science, 31*, 122–138.

Masuda, Y. (1981). *The information society as post-industrial society.* Bethesda, MD: World Future Society.

Matthews, J. R. (1980). *Choosing an automated library system: A planning guide.* Chicago: American Library Association.

Maule, R. W. (1994). Current information infrastructure policy in the United States. *Knowledge and Policy: The International Journal of Knowledge Transfer and Utilization, 7*, 17–30.

Means, R. (1983). The same old song. In W. Churchill (Ed.), *Marxism and Native Americans* (pp. 19–34). Boston: South End Press.

Meijer, J. G. (1982). *Librarianship: A definition.* Occasional Paper 155. Champaign-Urbana: University of Illinois Graduate School of Library and Information Science.

Merkle, J. A. (1980). *Management and ideology: The legacy of the international scientific management movement.* Berkeley: University of California Press.

Meyrowitz, J. (1985). *No sense of place: The impact of electronic media on social behavior.* Oxford, U.K.: Oxford University Press.

Midgley, M. (1989). *Wisdom, information, and wonder: What is knowledge for?* London: Routledge.

Miliband, R. (1969). *The state in capitalist society: An analysis of the western system of power.* New York: Basic Books.

Mitcham, C. (1986). Computers: From ethos and ethics to mythos and religion. Notes on the new frontier between computers and philosophy. *Technology in Society, 8,* 171–201.

Mitchell, W. J. (1992). *The reconfigured eye: Visual truth in the post-photographic era.* Cambridge, MA: MIT Press.

Mitchell, W. J. (1995). *City of bits: Space, place, and the infobahn.* Cambridge, MA: MIT Press.

Moffett, W. (1990). 1989–1990, an age of transition. *College & Research Library News, 51,* 96–98.

Molholt, P. (1986). The information machine: A new challenge for librarians. *Library Journal, 111,* 47–52.

Molholt, P. (1988). Libraries and new technologies: Courting the cheshire cat. *Library Journal, 113,* 37–41.

Molz, R. K. (1966–67). The public custody of the high pornography. *American Scholar, 36,* 93–103.

Molz, R. K. (1976). *Federal policy and library support.* Cambridge, MA: MIT Press.

Morgall, J. M. (1993). *Technology sssessment: A feminist perspective.* Philadelphia: Temple University Press.

Morton, M. S. (Ed.). (1991). *The corporation of the 1990s: Information technology and organizational transformation.* Oxford, U.K.: Oxford University Press.

Mosco, V. (1982). *Pushbutton fantasies: Critical perspectives on videotex and information technology.* Norwood, NJ: Ablex.

Mosco, V. (1989). *The pay-per society: Computers and communication in the information age—essays in critical theory and public policy.* Norwood, NJ: Ablex.

Mowery, D. C., & Rosenberg, N. (1989). *Technology and the pursuit of economic growth.* Cambridge, U.K.: Cambridge University Press.

Musmann, K. (1978). Will their be a role for librarians and libraries in the Post-Industrial Society? *Libri, 28,* 228–234.

Naisbitt, J. (1982). *Megatrends: Ten new directions transforming our lives.* New York: Warner Books.

National Commission on Libraries and Information Science. (1975). *Towards a national program for library and information services: Goals for action.* Washington, DC: NCLIS.

National Commission on Libraries and Information Science. (1982). *Public sector/private sector interaction in providing information services.* Washington, DC: NCLIS.

Nelson, J. S., Megill, A., & McCloskey, D. N. (Eds.). (1987). *The rhetoric of the human sciences: Language and argument in scholarship and public affairs.* Madison: University of Wisconsin Press.

Nielsen, B. (1980). Online bibliographic searching and the deprofessionalization of librarianship. *Online Review, 4,* 215–223.

Nielsen, B. (1989). Allocating costs, thinking about values: The fee-or-free debate revisited. *Journal of Academic Librarianship, 15,* 211–217.

Noble, David. (1977). *America by design: Science, technology, and the rise of corporate capitalism.* New York: Alfred A. Knopf.

Noble, David. (1984). *Forces of production: A social history of industrial automation.* New York: Alfred A. Knopf.

Noble, Douglas. (1984). The underside of computer literacy. *Raritan, 3,* 37–64.

NRENAISSANCE Committee. (1994). *Realizing the information future: The internet and beyond.* Washington, DC: National Academy Press.

Nunberg, G. (Ed.). (1996). *The future of the book.* Berkeley: University of California Press.

Nye, D. E. (1990). *Electrifying America: Social meanings of a new technology.* Cambridge, MA: MIT Press.

O'Connor, J. (1973). *The fiscal crisis of the state.* New York: St. Martin's.

Office of Technology Assessment (Congress of the United States). (1994). *Electronic enterprises: Looking to the future.* Washington, DC: Government Printing Office.

Ong, W. J. (1967). *The presence of the word.* New Haven, CT: Yale University Press.

Ong, W. J. (1982). *Orality and literacy: The technologizing of the word.* London: Methuen.

Ong, W. J. (1986). Writing is a technology that restructures thought. In G. Baumann (Ed.), *The written word: Literacy in transition,* (pp. 23–50). Oxford: Oxford University Press.

Pacey, A. (1983). *The culture of technology.* Cambridge, MA: MIT Press.

Pacey, A. (1990). *Technology in world civilization.* Cambridge, MA: MIT Press.

Park, B. (1992, Oct.). Libraries without walls; or, librarians without a profession. *American Libraries* 746–747.

Patterson, L. R., & Lindberg, S. W. (1991). *The nature of copyright: A law of user's rights.* Athens: University of Georgia Press.

Pattison, R. (1982). *On literacy: The politics of the word from Homer to the age of rock.* Oxford, U.K.: Oxford University Press.

Pavlik, J. V. (1996). *New media and the information superhighway.* Boston: Allyn and Bacon.

Peek, R. P., & Burstyn, J. N. (1991). The pursuit of improved scholarly publications. In J. N. Burstyn (Ed.), *Desktop publishing in the university* (pp. 99–120). Syracuse, NY: Syracuse University Press.

Peek, R. P., & Newby, G. B. (Eds.). (1996). *Scholarly publishing: The electronic frontier.* Cambridge, MA: MIT Press.

Pemberton, J. M., & Nugent, C. R. (1995). Information studies: Emergent field, convergent curriculum. *Journal of Education for Library and Information Science, 36,* 126–138.

Perrolle, J. A. (1991). Intellectual assembly lines: The rationalization of managerial, professional, and technical work. In C. Dunlop & R. Kling (Eds.), *Computerization and controversy: Value conflicts and social choice* (pp. 111–122). San Diego, CA: Academic Press.

Perry, R., & Greber, L. (1990). Women and computers: An introduction. *Signs, 16,* 74–101.

Peters, P. E. (1995, March 15). Information age avatars. *Library Journal,* 33–34.

Petroski, H. (1990). *The pencil: A history of design and circumstance.* New York: Alfred Knopf.

Pool, I. de Sola. (1982). The culture of electronic print. *Daedalus, 111,* 17–31.

Pool, I. de Sola. (1983). *Technologies of freedom: On free speech in an electronic age.* Cambridge, MA: Harvard University Press.

Pool, I. de Sola. (1990). *Technologies without boundaries: On telecommunications in a global age.* Cambridge, MA: Harvard University Press.

Porat, M. U. (1977). *The information economy.* Report Series in 9 volumes. Washington, DC: U. S. Department of Commerce, Office of Telecommunications.

Porat, M. U. (1978). Emergence of an information economy. *Economic Impact, 4,* 29–34.

Poster, M. (1990). *The mode of information: Poststructuralism and social context.* Chicago: University of Chicago Press.

Pritchard, S. (1993, Fall). Feminist thought and the critique of information technology. *Progressive Librarian,* 1–9.

Public Library Association, Goals, Guidelines and Standards Committee. (1977). A mission statement for public libraries: Guidelines for public library service, Part 1. *American Libraries, 8,* 615–20.

Rakow, L. K. (1988). Gendered technology, gendered practice. *Critical Studies in Mass Communication, 5,* 57–70.

Reeves, W. J. (1980). *Librarians as professionals: The occupation's impact on library work arrangements.* Lexington, MA: Lexington Books.

Regan, P. M. (1995). *Legislating privacy: Technology, social values, and public policy.* Chapel Hill: University of North Carolina Press.

Reskin, B. (1988). Bringing the men back in: Sex differentiation and the devaluation of women's work. *Gender and Society, 2,* 58–81.

Rider, F. (1944). *The scholar and the future of the research library: A Problem and its solution.* New York: Hadham

Riedinger, E. A. (1989). "Information Age" as a descriptor. *Scholarly Publishing, 21,* 45–51.

Rifkin, J. (1995). *The end of work: The decline of the global labor force and the dawn of the post-market era.* New York: Tarcher/Putnam.

Ring, D. F. (1996, January/February). The librarian as a "bookman." *Public Libraries,* 60–63.

Robins, K., & Webster, F. (1987). Information as capital: A critique of Daniel Bell. In J. Slack & F. Fejes (Eds.), *The ideology of the information age,* (pp. 95–117). Norwood, NJ: Ablex.

Rochell, C. (1985). The knowledge business: Economic issues of access to bibliographic information. *College & Research Libraries, 46,* 5–12.

Rochell, C. (1987). The next decade: Distributed access to information. *Library Journal, 112,* 42-48.

Rodgers, D. T. (1987). *Contested truths: Keywords in American politics since independence.* New York: Basic Books.

Rogers, E. M. (1986). *Communication technology: The new media in society.* New York: Free Press.

Rose, M. A. (1991). *The post-modern and the post-industrial: A critical analysis.* Cambridge, U.K.: Cambridge University Press.

Ross, A. (1989). *No respect: Intellectuals and popular culture.* London: Routledge.

Ross, A. (1991). Hacking away at the counterculture. In C. Penley & A. Ross (Eds.), *Technoculture,* (pp. 107-134). Minneapolis: University of Minnesota Press.

Ross, G. (1974). The second coming of Daniel Bell. *Socialist Register,* 331–348.

Roszak, T. (1986). *The cult of information: The folklore of computers and the true art of thinking.* New York: Pantheon.

Said, E. W. (1983). Opponents, audiences, constituencies and community. In H. Foster (Ed.), *The anti-aesthetic: Essays on postmodern culture* (pp. 135–159). Port Townsend, WA: Bay Press.

Sale, K. (1995). *Rebels against the future: Lessons for the computer age.* New York: Addison-Wesley.

Savitch, H. V. (1988). *Post-industrial cities: Politics and planning in New York, Paris, and London.* Princeton, NJ: Princeton University Press.

Schauder, D. (1994). Electronic publishing of professional articles: Attitudes of academics and implications for the scholarly communication industry. *Journal of the American Society for Information Science, 45,* 73–100.

Schement, J. R. (1996, May 1). A 21st-century strategy for librarians. *Library Journal,* 34–36.

Schiller, A. (1981). Shifting boundaries of information. *Library Journal* 106, 706–709.

Schiller, D. 1988. How to think about information. In V. Mosco & J. Wasko (Eds.), *The Political Economy of Information* (pp. 27–43). Madison: University of Wisconsin Press.

Schiller, H. (1996). *Information inequality: The deepening social crisis in America.* London: Routledge.

Schiller, H., & Schiller, A. (1988). Libraries, public access to information, and commerce. In V. Mosco & J. Wasko (Eds.), *The political economy of information* (pp. 146–166). Madison: University of Wisconsin Press.

Schlesinger, A. M., Jr. (1986). *The cycles of American history.* New York: Houghton, Mifflin.

Schon, D. A. (1979). Generative metaphor: A perspective on problem setting in social policy. In A. Ortony (Ed.), *Metaphor and thought* (pp. 254–283). Cambridge, U.K.: Cambridge University Press.

Schroyer, T. (1974). Review of the coming of Post-Industrial Society. *Telos, 19,* 162–176.

Schuman, P. G. (1982). Information justice: A review of the NCLIS report. *Library Journal, 107,* 1060–1066.

Schuman, P. G. (1990). Reclaiming our technological future. *Library Journal, 115,* 34–38.

Schumpeter, J. A. (1950). *Capitalism, socialism, and democracy.* (3rd ed.). New York: Harper and Brothers.

Sculley, J. (1991). The relationship between business and higher education: A perspective on the 21st century. In C. Dunlop & R. Kling (Eds.), *Computerization and controversy: Value conflicts and social choices* (pp. 55–62). San Diego, CA: Academic Press.

Segal, H. P. (1985). *Technological utopianism in American culture.* Chicago: University of Chicago Press.

Seiler, L., & Surprenant, T. (1991). When we get the libraries we want, will we want the libraries we get? *Wilson Library Bulletin, 65,* 29–31, 152, 157.

Shamp, S. A. (1992). Prospects for electronic publication in communication: A survey of potential users. *Communication Quarterly, 40,* 297–304.

Shapiro, I. (1986). *The evolution of rights in liberal theory.* Cambridge, U.K.: Cambridge University Press.

Shapiro, I. (1990). *Political criticism.* Berkeley: University of California Press.

Siegel, L., & Markoff, J. (1985). *The high cost of high tech: The dark side of the chip.* New York: Harper and Row.

Slack, J. (1984). *Communication technologies and society: Conceptions of causality and the politics of technological intervention.* Norwood, NJ: Ablex.

Smith, B. (1989). A strategic approach to online user fees in public libraries. *Library Journal, 114,* 33–36.

Smith, D. (1985). The commercialization and privatization of government information. *Government Publications Review, 12,* 45–63.

Smith, H. J. (1994). *Managing privacy: Information technology and corporate America.* Chapel Hill: University of North Carolina Press.

Smith, M. R., & Marx, L. (Eds.). (1994). *Does technology drive history? The dilemma of technological determinism.* Cambridge, MA: MIT Press.

Sosa, J., & Harris, M. H. (1991). José Ortega y Gasset and the role of the librarian in Post-industrial America. *Libri, 41,* 3–21.

Sprehe, T. J. (1994). Federal information policy in the Clinton administration's first year. *Bulletin of the Ameican Society for Information Science, 20,* 20–25.

Starr, P. (1988). The meaning of privatization. *Yale Law and Policy Review, 6,* 6–41.

Steinfels, P. (1979). *The neoconservatives: The men who are changing America's politics.* New York: Simon & Schuster.

Stielow, F. (1983). Censorship in the early professionalization of American libraries, 1876–1929. *Journal of Library History, 18,* 37–54.

St. Lifer, E., & Rogers, M. (1994, May 1). Public interest groups flock to D. C. to discuss shaping NII. *Library Journal,* 14–15.

Stoffle, C. J., Renaud, R., & Veldof, J. R. (1996). Choosing our futures. *College & Research Libraries, 57,* 213–225.

Stone, A. R. (1995). *The war of desire and technology at the close of the mechanical age.* Cambridge, MA: MIT Press.

Strassmann, P. A. (1985). *Information payoff: The transformation of work in the electronic age.* New York: Free Press.

Sullivan, W. M. (1995). *Work and integrity: The crisis and promise of professionalism in America.* New York: Harper Business.

Surprenant, T. (1982). Future libraries. *Wilson Library Bulletin, 56,* 152–153.

Swan, J. (1988). Information and madness. *Library Journal, 113,* 25–28.

Tapscott, D. (1996). *The digital economy: Promise and peril in the age of networked intelligence.* New York: McGraw-Hill.

Taylor, R. S. (1975). Patterns toward a user-centered academic library. In E. J. Josey (Ed.). *New dimensions for academic library service* (pp. 298–304). Metuchen, NJ: Scarecrow Press.

Tenopir, C. (1995). Authors and readers: The keys to success or failure for electronic publishing. *Library Trends, 43,* 571–591.

Theim, J. (1979). The great library of Alexandria burnt: Towards the history of a symbol. *Journal of the History of Ideas, 40*, 507–526.

Thompson, J. (1982). *The end of libraries*. London: Clive Bingley.

Thompson, W. I. (1989). *Imaginary landscape: Making worlds of myth and science*. New York: St. Martin's.

Tichi, C. (1987). *Shifting gears: Technology, literature, culture in modernist America*. Chapel Hill: University of North Carolina Press.

Toffler, A. (1980). *The third wave*. New York: William Morrow.

Turkle, S. (1995). *Life on the screen: Identity in the age of the internet*. New York: Simon & Schuster.

Turock, B. (1994, Feb. 15). The new case for federal library support. *Library Journal*, 126–128.

Vagianos, L., & Lesser, B. (1990). Information policy issues: Putting library policy in context. In *Rethinking the library in the information age*, (Vol. 2). (pp. 9–39). Washington, DC: Government Printing Office.

Valaskakis, K. (1982). The concept of informediation: A framework for a structural interpretation of the information revolution. In L. Bannon, U. Barry, & O. Holst (Eds.), *Information technology: Impact on the way of life*, (pp. 21–36). Dublin, Ireland: Tycooly Publishing.

Vann, S. K. (ed.), (1978). *Melvil Dewey: His enduring presence in librarianship*. Littleton, CO: Libraries Unlimited.

Veaner, A. B. (1985). 1985 to 1995: The next decade in academic librarianship, Part I. *College & Research Libraries, 46*, 209–229.

Veysey, L. (1982). A postmortem on Daniel Bell's postindustrialism. *American Quarterly, 34*, 49–69.

Wagner, J. (1979). Defining technology: Political implications of hardware, software, power, and information. *Human Relations, 32*, 719–736.

Wajcman, J. (1991). Patriarchy, technology, and conceptions of skill. *Work and Occupations, 18*, 29–45.

Wasserman, P. (1972). *The new librarianship: A challenge for change*. New York: Bowker.

Webster, F., & Robins, K. (1986). *Information technology: A Luddite analysis*. Norwood, NJ: Ablex.

Wiegand, W. A. (1996). *Irrepressible reformer: A biography of Melvil Dewey*. Chicago: American Library Association.

Weisbrod, B. A. (1988). *The nonprofit economy*. Cambridge, MA: Harvard University Press.

Wilensky, H. L. (1964). The professionalization of everyone? *American Journal of Sociology*, (70), 137–158.

Williams, C. L. (1995). *Still a man's world: Men who do women's work*. Berkeley: University of California Press.

Williams P., & Pearce, J. T. (1978). *The vital network: A theory of communication and society*. Westport, CT: Greenwood.

Wilson, K. (1988). *Technologies of control: The new interactive media for the home*. Madison: University of Wisconsin Press.

Wilson, Patrick. (1977). *Public knowledge, private ignorance: Toward a library and information Policy*. Westport, CT: Greenwood.

Wilson, Pauline. (1978). Librarianship and ALA in a post-industrial society. *American Libraries, 9,* 124–128.

Wilson, Pauline. (1982). *Stereotype and status: Librarians in the United States.* Westport, CT: Greenwood.

Winner, L. (1977). *Autonomous technology: Technics-out-of-control as a theme in political thought.* Cambridge, MA: MIT Press.

Winner, L. (1986). Mythinformation. In L. Winner (Ed.), *The whale and the reactor: A search for limits in an age of high technology* (pp. 98–117). Chicago: University of Chicago Press.

Winston, B. (1986). *Misunderstanding media.* Cambridge, MA: Harvard University Press.

Winston, B. (1989). The illusion of revolution. In T. Forester (Ed.), *Computers in the human context: Information technology, productivity and people* (pp. 71–81). Cambridge, MA: MIT Press.

Winter, M. (1988). *The culture and control of expertise: Toward a sociological understanding of librarianship.* Westport, CT: Greenwood.

Wittig, R. (1994). *Invisible rendezvous: Connection and collaboration in the new landscape of electronic writing.* Hanover, NH: Weslyan University Press.

Wolfe, A. (1993). *The human difference: Animals, computers, and the necessity of social science.* Berkeley: University of California Press.

Woodsworth, A. (1989). The model research library: Planning for the future. *Journal of Academic Librarianship, 15,* 132–138.

Woodward, K. (Ed.). (1980). *The myths of information: Technology and postindustrial culture.* Madison: Coda Press for the University of Wisconsin.

Wresch, W. (1996). *Disconnected: Haves and have-nots in the information age.* New Brunswick, NJ: Rutgers University Press.

Wriston, W. (1992). *The twilight of sovereignty: How the information revolution is transforming our world.* New York: Scribners.

Zimmerman, J. (Ed.). (1983). *The technological women.* New York: Praeger.

Zuboff, S. (1988). *In the age of the smart machine: The future of work and power.* New York: Basic Books.

Zukin, S. (1991). *Landscapes of power: From Detroit to Disney World.* Berkeley: University of California Press.

Author Index

Subject Index